START A SUCCESSFUL BUSINESS

START A SUCCESSFUL BUSINESS

Rosemary Phipps

BBC BOOKS

Published by BBC Books,
a division of BBC Enterprises Limited,
Woodlands, 80 Wood Lane
London W12 0TT

First Published 1994

© Rosemary Phipps 1994
ISBN 0 563 36962 0
Designed by Gwyn Lewis

Typeset in Great Britain by
Phoenix Photosetting, Chatham, Kent
Printed and bound in Great Britain by
Clays Ltd, St Ives plc
Cover printed by Clays Ltd, St Ives plc

Contents

Acknowledgements

I wish to acknowledge the work done by the Grubb Institute and the Tavistock Clinic in London on the concept of role, and Isabel Menzies Lyth for her work on institutional defences.

I would like to thank my colleagues at Oxford College of Further Education: Christopher Gowers for his detailed help on the law, M. Hussein Mirza for his help on break-even analysis, profit and loss, and the balance sheet, and Tyrell Gillman for casting a professional eye over the text. Last, but not least, I would like to thank David Holt and my two children Sophie and William who have provided so much support, and Jean Collard for being a true friend.

Note: The cases used as examples in this book are built up from a range of fairly typical case histories. In no way do they relate to specific people.

Introduction

Are you ready to start your own business ?

The successes and failures of entrepreneurs tend to awaken a sense of excitement in all of us. Their ability to project ideas and bring money, skills and markets together into a tangible reality makes them the folk heroes of today. The entrepreneur is the person who after many hardships, trials and adventures seems finally to make it: the Prometheus or Odysseus of the modern world.

Sadly, success may lead to hubris and a tragic fall. The histories of many entrepreneurs show that success is a fragile state and one that can easily be followed by failure. Nevertheless small firms play an important part in our economy, both in creating jobs and providing competition and innovation. In Great Britain such firms account for a smaller proportion of employment than is the case with many of our foreign competitors. However there is no reason why they should not become a more substantial sector within our economy.

Knowing all this, you need to ask yourself some searching questions: Do I really want to run my own business? Am I an entrepreneur? Could I become one? What is it like and what do I have to do? How can I find out? How can I start my own business and not make a fool of myself?

This book describes the steps you need to take in order to succeed. Don't make the mistakes that others have made before. Find out how to free the entrepreneur in you in the safest possible way.

Throughout this book there are references to agencies and organizations that you may need to contact. You will find their details in the 'Useful addresses' section on p. 172.

The most frequent references are to the two organizations that have been specifically set up to help new businesses – the Training and Enterprise Council (TEC) and the Enterprise Agency. You will find their nearest offices in your local telephone directory.

1 How to find a good business idea

The first step is to find a product to manufacture or an idea for one, or you might decide to provide a service or go into distribution. Although your choice will partly depend on your skills and interests, it must also provide what customers are looking for. Try and choose something that you will enjoy selling and that there is a demand for. Some people find it easier to sell ideas, other people find it easier to sell goods. Really think about this, because your passion and enthusiasm for your work will communicate itself to potential customers and help you succeed. Some ideas may give you a buzz, others may not seem quite so appealing. For example, if you can't stand the smell of fish, it's obviously not a good idea to open a fish and chip shop. Your staff may get ill and you'll be left holding the pan!

Most ideas are not original. When you look at an idea you need to think about how to differentiate your version from those of your competitors (don't over-exaggerate the differences, otherwise your customers may feel uneasy). As soon as you start thinking about it you will find there are masses of ideas around. Most business ideas come from taking somebody else's idea and adapting it. The idea might be redesigned and made to do more, or less. Or it could be made smaller, bigger, cheaper, more expensive, or it might be produced in a different colour or the presentation or promotional methods could be changed. When you look at the market choose something in which you can create a niche for yourself and then think about how you can improve on it by adding extra value. Emphasize the specialist nature of your business and don't try to be 'all things to all men'.

Look at the market first

It is better to look at the market first and then decide on the best way to earn a living. There are plenty of ideas about but finding a profitable idea and one that customers want, and a business that you will enjoy running, may not be that easy. You may need to look, or at least be prepared to look, at several ideas before you even start. This will help you keep an open mind and assess things rationally rather than getting over-attached to an idea just because you like it. Be led by the market, not only by what you want to do. Look at all business ideas from your customers' viewpoint.

A good idea must make money for you. It must therefore be something that people want and it must also sell at a price your customers are willing to pay. People will often say 'What a good idea' or 'I like that!', but when it comes to paying for it . . . well, that's another matter. You must research your market carefully.

Decide how much to invest

Some businesses start off in a small way, with a minimum of capital outlay; others require a greater capital investment. You should work out how much you can afford to risk financially. You also need to think about your objectives from the very beginning. For example, if you only want to make a comfortable living don't choose something that is going to require endless effort and growth in order to expand and survive. Read Chapter 13 on 'Managing yourself' and be honest about what you really want to achieve and are able to manage.

Be patient

Some ideas take a long time to put into action, especially ones which involve finding premises and clearing planning permission. It may also take a long time to get your business established –

customers may need to build up their trust in you before they can start putting orders your way. On average you'll have to call on people six times before you get the business. This is not a job for the faint-hearted! It's best to start trying out your ideas part-time. If possible, cut down on the amount of work you're doing in your full-time job; and instead of watching television in the evenings you can start researching and developing your own ideas.

There are no short cuts to success

Don't be caught out by the promise of easy riches or by magazine articles telling you how easy it will all be. Before you start, check your ideas and work out your costs carefully. Once you have assessed your first idea thoroughly, you may have to find another. There may be too much competition, there may not be enough customers, it may require too much advertising, take too long to recoup your investment, or just not be profitable enough. Don't get too attached to any of your ideas before you have assessed them thoroughly.

Getting attached to an idea is rather like falling in love – it is often the sense of fantasy and potential bliss that drives you on rather than the reality and it is very easy to lose your sense of perspective. When you're in love with a particular person it is difficult to remember that there are still other people out there, waiting for you to discover them. It is the same with ideas.

Match your skills to your business idea

If you're considering an idea in a totally different area from your present work, it is a good idea to continue with your current job for at least a few months. Although the actual tasks may be similar, it takes time to absorb the work culture in a different field.

While it is important to know something about the area in which you intend to work, or at least to have a feel for it, most skills are learnt 'on the job'. It is only by doing them that you really learn. However if you are going to be a gardener you obviously have to know the difference between a flower and a weed, and if you are going to be a builder you must know how to build – you will only lose your customers if you produce shoddy work.

Pat wanted to go into publishing. She liked the idea but knew nothing about the mechanics of producing a book. She wrote a book and was about to get it printed when she happened to talk, quite by chance, to a publisher. He suggested she take the book to a copy-editor. Much to her surprise, when the manuscript came back, she found that it had been corrected. There were all sorts of errors, ranging from sentence construction and spelling to syntax and punctuation. She had never felt so humiliated in her life. And that was only the beginning. By the time she had worked her way through the problems of design, proof-reading and colour printing she had learnt a lot about publishing, but it was a very stressful and expensive way of learning. Mind you, she never made the same mistakes again.

Get the right skills

You may find something you would like to do, but realize that you lack one or more of the basic skills to carry it out. It is usually cheaper to buy-in the skill, rather than risk making a mess of it yourself, especially if you really can't do it or don't have the time to do it well.

In some cases you will have to consider specific training. It could even be worth working without pay for a short period, helping out in a business in which you are interested. Even if you plan to stick to what you know already, you will still need to get advice on running a business. There are plenty of courses around – ask at your local Training and Enterprise Council (TEC).

Different types of ideas

Here are some different types of ideas to consider:

Small markets

Some small companies do well by capturing a small market that the larger companies are uninterested in, perhaps for the following reasons:

- The larger companies have rationalized their businesses and are no longer interested in the smaller segments (e.g. some parts of the bread, cake and ice-cream market).

- The larger companies find it difficult to react quickly to frequent variations in demand and taste (e.g. in women's clothing and other fashion items).

- The larger companies supply standardized products and there is a demand for originality (e.g. in shopfitting, or kitchen and bedroom design).

- The market may be very fragmented, with a large number of customers who want different things (e.g. custom-made machine parts).

■ Retailing

Retailing will always require an investment of capital in order to buy or lease property and buy initial stock. You will also need some managerial skills. However there are certain types of shops that are easier to succeed in for various reasons. It is a good idea to look out for retail businesses with one or more of the following:

- Long anti-social hours (e.g. newsagents, greengrocers, tobacconists and newsagents, florists).

- A stock of a large number of different products (e.g. gift shops, jewellery, china and glassware, and delicatessens).

- Resale price maintenance so that you do not have to compete with the larger firms in price wars (e.g. bookshops and newsagents).

- Businesses where you need to have a highly trained and specialist salesforce who know a lot about the products (e.g. bicycles, antiques and photography).

- Businesses where you need to be very flexible and offer a good after-sales service (e.g. hire and repair and soft furnishings).

- Businesses where you can offer a competitive advantage (e.g. a grocer who can offer a delivery service).

- A geographical area where larger companies have closed down their small and medium-sized shops.

■ **Franchising**

This can be a good way of finding a business idea because it removes some of the risks. What you will be doing is taking on an idea that the franchiser has already tested commercially. You then pay for the right to use the business name and pay the franchiser a royalty fee based on your sales. You have probably heard of the larger franchise organizations such as Wimpy and Prontaprint. There are many other smaller ones and the investment required will vary according to the business and its potential. It is a good idea to check all the details very carefully. Speak to other franchisees, read up on everything you can, and contact the British Franchise Association (see Useful addresses). Most banks now have someone who can give you advice on franchising as well.

■ **Import**

There has been an increase in the number of imported goods and many home markets have collapsed because of increased competition from abroad, so importing could enable you to provide a product that is cheaper or better. Research your market thoroughly (whether you plan to sell via retailers or direct to customers), check freight costs, and contact the relevant embassies to ask about potential opportunities and problems.

■ **Export**

On 1 January 1993 the single European market was declared 'open for business'. There is now a single market of 340 million potential customers with routine customs clearance of commercial goods. Although these changes have made trading in Europe easier there are still differences in the way goods and services are presented to different nationalities and also in business practice and style. The Department of Trade and Industry's publication, entitled *Business in Europe*, (see Useful addresses), offers practical advice to help businesses compete successfully in Europe.

Only you can decide how best to exploit these new opportunities. There are great opportunities for businesses and also great threats, as European businesses seek to extend their activities in Great Britain.

If you're thinking of Europe it is no good treating the market there as an optional extra. You'll need to get information on Value Added Tax (VAT), market research and consumer tastes and many other aspects. Your local Training and Enterprise Council office should put you into touch with local networks.

■ **Matching agency**
If you have some money which you would like to use to start a business, but are unsure about what sort of business you want to go into, it is a good idea to contact a matching agency which will find a suitable business idea for you. Alternatively, if you are sure you have a good idea but not enough money or experience to develop it to its proper potential you could try contacting Venture Capital Report Limited and the Local Investment Networking Company (see Useful addresses).

■ **Selling**
People with experience in selling can try contacting the Manufacturers' Agents Association and the British Agents Register (see Useful addresses). These organizations will put you in touch with manufacturers and suppliers who cannot afford to employ a permanent salesforce of their own and may be interested in taking on a freelance representative. Other manufacturers may be dealing with a very fragmented market and it might be more cost-effective for them to place their goods with representatives who are carrying more than one line.

■ **Manufacturing**
If you have capital and the right skills it is possible to run a small manufacturing firm profitably. However you will need to have sufficient spare, or risk, capital to invest in buildings, machines, tools and raw materials. You will also need to know about marketing, sales, distribution, financial control and managing people. If you have thought up an original idea but you don't want

to deal with the whole business yourself, you might be able to find a business to take on certain aspects (e.g. invoicing and distribution). Another option is to try and find someone with whom you can pool resources – perhaps sharing office space, fax or photocopying facilities, or secretarial help.

Do remember to protect any new ideas before telling any interested party about it. (See p. 69 for information on patent and copyright.)

■ **Services**
This is a growing area and one that is worth investigating thoroughly. People *experience* services, so think about how you can make your service really enjoyable to use. Concentrate on intangible aspects (such as quality and efficiency) and how you can make them solid and measurable. It is possible to start a service business with only a small outlay of capital and with very little risk of losing your money. However, many of the opportunities may be local and your success will very much depend on what is already available in your area. Do be careful if it is an area that has attracted a number of part-timers (e.g. window cleaning or house cleaning) since the low-priced competition may make it difficult to earn a living. However, if a product has a generic quality to it, like cleaning, it is possible to differentiate yourself so that people will perceive you as being different.

Here are some examples of services you could provide:

- Business services (e.g. typing, computer training, word-processing, book-keeping, insurance, office cleaning and recruitment).

- Publishing, writing and editorial services (e.g. desktop publishing, editorial work such as copy-editing and proof-reading, copy-writing, design and illustration).

- Home services (e.g. gardening, plumbing, building, painting and decorating, house letting, property management, window cleaning and domestic cleaning).

- Professional services (e.g. dentistry, optometry, business management, consultancy, advertising, marketing, market research, product development, education and training).

- Personal services (e.g. home hairdressing, massage, exercise, photography, counselling and psychotherapy).

- Theatre, radio, television and film.

■ **Catering**
This area covers a variety of products and services, including:

- Running your own take-away food outlet.

- Running your own café or restaurant.

- Providing meals for companies and executive lunches.

- Supplying food to pubs, bars, clubs and hotels.

- Catering for parties.

For detailed information contact the Hotel and Catering Industry Training Board (see Useful addresses) or your local Tourist Board.

■ **Publications**
There are publications which describe products or processes which are available for licensing. Newspapers often carry advertisements for business opportunities and you can ask at your local library for books carrying this information. The British Library, Science Reference and Information Service (see Useful addresses) may have copies of these publications: *Prestwick Publications, Venture Product News, Mintel Publications, Euromonitor Publications.* And if you read French or can get it translated you could write to: Idées Lucratives, Editions Selz, 1 Place du Lycee, B.P. 266 68005 COLMAR CEDIX, France.

■ **Joint ventures**
Larger businesses are often happy to work with smaller companies or self-employed people who can provide them with particular skills such as developing ideas, running projects and so on. These skills might be required on an ongoing basis or could be called in when there is a demand. The methods of payment differ. Some people are paid a retainer; others will have an overall contract with

no retainer but are called in to carry out specific pieces of work when the need arises. You have to seek out these opportunities for yourself, though your existing employer might be a good starting point. It is sometimes possible to continue doing a similar job on a freelance basis.

Whatever your choice and however large you intend your business to be, make sure that you are always at the proverbial 'coal face'. Keep in touch with your customers, listen to them, respond to them quickly, be flexible, and make sure you give them a high quality product – eat, sleep and drink quality. You must always know what they want. Constantly ask yourself: 'How can I provide a better service, a better product?'. You must be passionate about your idea and always think about how you can improve on it – because if you don't, somebody else will: that is the nature of the market.

2 How to develop your idea

In order to develop your business idea and your marketing strategy you first need to develop an outline of what you want to do and then research it.

The marketing mix

You will reach your customers by using what is called the marketing mix. The marketing mix consists of: product/service, promotion (advertising, selling, sales promotion and public relations), price, and the place you sell from. You blend these together to meet the needs and requirements of a particular group or groups of people. These elements are commonly referred to as the 4Ps – Product, Promotion, Price, Place.

You can add another three Ps (making 7Ps) if you're a service – People (anyone in contact with customers, even the customers themselves), Physical Evidence (the actual objects used in providing the service and the atmosphere they create) and the Process (the sequence, capacity and its quality control).

In practice most products purchased entail some element of service (e.g. delivery, credit) and most services have tangible elements (e.g. packaging).

How to develop your outline

1. Decide exactly which business you are in so that you can look at the market and identify your competitors.

2. Choose which segment/segments of the market you are going for. This means understanding who your customers will be.

3. Find out exactly what your customers want, and work out how to give it to them by using the right marketing mix (the 4Ps or 7Ps).

4. Think about how to reach or get your product/service to your target market.

How to select (segment) your market

Having decided on roughly the area you want to get into, you then need to refine your ideas. You may have to extend what you are offering or look at different segments of the market.

Market segmentation is a way of classifying customers into different groups of people with different needs and characteristics and different ways of behaving. A market segment is made up of people who respond in a similar way to a given set of market stimuli, so that your publicity material, your product/service and the place you're selling from will affect them all in more or less the same way.

This means that you must tailor your product/service, corporate image and marketing mix so that your customers recognize that the product/service exists specifically for them. When asked who their customers are, many new entrepreneurs say: 'People', 'Everybody', or 'We'll know when we start' or 'We'll see who they are when we put our first advertisement in the newspaper'. This is a misguided approach. No business can appeal to everyone. It is therefore essential to have a clear idea of who your customers are before you begin.

Markets consist of buyers, and buyers differ in a number of ways. This makes each set of buyers into a potentially different and separate market because each set has their own unique needs, tastes, lifestyle, cultural background, attitude towards products/ services and also towards the way in which they purchase.

You will do better if you appeal to certain segments only, which means identifying which part of the market you can serve best and most profitably. This is called target marketing.

Once you have evaluated the segments and decided whether you will go for one, or more than one, you will have to position yourself within each segment. The position you take will depend on what your competitors are offering. A position is the place a product occupies in the consumer's mind relative to that of your competitors. Your product/service must occupy a clear, distinctive and desirable place in the minds of your customers – you must differentiate yourself. If you're aiming to target more than one segment it is easy to get confused, so it's advisable to follow the procedure described in this chapter.

There is no single way to segment a market and each of you will have to reach your own way of describing your customers. But for any new business you will need to begin with the seven stages described below:

■ **Stage One**
First think of the major groups of people who are likely to buy your product/service.

■ **Stage Two**
Underneath that, assign a percentage to each segment in terms of the business you expect to get from each group of customers.

■ **Stage Three**
Then think about your product/service and decide which features you will provide for each segment.

■ **Stage Four**
Write down the benefits each segment will get from purchasing those features.

■ **Stage Five**
Now decide on an appropriate price for each segment you are selling to.

■ **Stage Six**
Now decide on an appropriate method of promotion for each segment you are selling to.

■ **Stage Seven**

Write down the place or places you will be selling from.

These stages are considered in more detail below.

■ **Stage One   Customer segmentation**

The first step is to think about the characteristics of your potential customers, remembering that you'll probably use more than one set of characteristics. Consider:

- Where they live geographically (country, urban, suburban, rural, climate).

- What their demographic characteristics are (income, age, sex, family size, stage in life). The theory here is that people have different aspirations and behaviour patterns as they go through their life cycle. You could also look at education, race, nationality, religion, residence and social grade (as defined in Table 1 below).

- What their lifestyle is like (values, attitude, self-image, culture, personality traits).

- How often they are likely to purchase and use your product/service (by volume and frequency).

Table 1

This table defines social grade and class according to occupation.

Social Grade	Social Status	Occupation
A	Upper middle class	Higher managerial, administrative or professional.
B	Middle class	Intermediate managerial, administrative or professional.
C1	Lower middle class	Supervisory or clerical, junior managerial, administrative or professional.

C2	Skilled working class	Skilled manual workers.	
D	Working class	Semi- and unskilled manual workers.	
E	Those at lowest level of subsistence	State pensioners or widows (no other earner), casual or lowest-grade workers.	

Table 2

This table indicates the numerical strength of each social grade in Great Britain, as measured in 1991.

Social Grade	All Adults 15 +	
	'000's	%
A	1,307	2.9
B	6,799	15.0
C1	10,970	24.2
C2	12,278	27.1
D	7,939	17.5
E	5,958	13.2

Note: These social grades are based on heads of household.

Source: National Readership Survey July 1991–June 1992.

The Marketing Pocket Book, 1993, published by the Advertising Association in association with NTC Publications (see Useful addresses). There are plenty of other relevant statistics in this excellent little book. You should also be able to get information on the population of your own locality from your Local Training and Enterprise Council office.

Segmentation is a powerful tool and will help you serve your customers, whether they are consumers or buyers for industry. If you are targeting industrial markets you will need to think about some additional factors, including:

- Their sales turnover and number of employees.

- How often they will use your product/service.

- The type of industry.

- The personal characteristics of the buyers.

And so it goes on – don't stop here.

■ **Stage Two   Percentage of the business**
Once you have segmented the market you'll need to decide how many segments to cover and how to identify the most profitable ones. Not all segments are of equal value, so identify the segment or segments where your greatest opportunities lie and concentrate on those. Look at each segment and try to estimate how much business you will get from each one. Assign a percentage to each segment. This is very important because it is quite easy to choose the wrong segment and end up concentrating your efforts on the least profitable section of the business. Refer back to this when you do your costings.

■ **Stage Three   Feature segmentation**
When you have finished segmenting your market, you may like to think a little more about the actual product or service you'll be providing. Some people decide to offer each segment a modified product or service. Other people provide the same features for all their segments. It depends on your business idea and your customers' requirements.

■ **Stage Four   Benefit segmentation**
The fourth stage is to focus on what principal benefit your customers are likely to want from your product/service. Focus on what you think people will want from you and then consider whether you can meet their requirements. This is difficult to do, as it is almost impossible to see something from another person's point of view. Many people find themselves writing down a list of

features rather than benefits. If you find yourself doing this try turning it around and saying to yourself, 'which means that. . .'.

EXAMPLES

- Triumph Dandruff Shampoo contains X12. X12 is a feature which means that you will not be troubled by white flecks on your shoulders (benefit), which means that you'll automatically become devastatingly attractive (benefit)!

- When people buy a holiday to a hot country in the middle of winter, what benefits do they get? The answers could be any of these: romance, fun, a tan, night life, duty-free goods, sun, sand and sex, a rest.

- When people buy a motor car, what benefits do they get? Safety, speed, convenience, comfort, an image, higher status.

- A steel drill is made of first class steel (a feature) but this means that it can make a perfect hole (a benefit). What people want is a quality product that produces a perfect hole.

Ideas need translating, otherwise people say, 'So what?'. If someone said, 'I am a consultant', this would mean very little to most people. However if the person said, 'I can help you make more money', this would have a lot more impact. Help people think things through to reach the real feelings and reasons behind their purchasing.

■ **Stage Five   Price segmentation**
It is important to start thinking about your pricing and what you could charge customers in each segment. For example, if you were a management trainer and you sold your services to a college, you would probably be paid at a rate of just over £22 an hour. However if you sold the same training yourself direct to businesses you could be paid between £300 and £800 a day.

Up to a point, your market will dictate your prices and most initial prices and costings will later need to be changed, but at this stage it is useful to start thinking about them in relation to your market segments. Refer back to this when you do your costings and work out your final prices.

■ **Stage Six   Promotion segmentation**
Different segments may require different methods of promotion.

■ **Stage Seven   Place segmentation**
Reflect on how you can reach your different segments. You may be selling from the same place, but on the other hand, you may be able to reach them through different distribution channels.

Now draw your segmentation grid (add more columns if you need them for each segment).

	Segment 1	*Segment 2*	*Segment 3*
1. Segment/s Name the segment/s you're going into.	. . . .	. . . .	. . . .
2. Percentage of business Write down the percentage of business you can expect to get from each segment. (When you do your research, if you can, write down the percentage of business that you think comes from each of these segments nationally. How does your choice match up with these? Have you chosen the most profitable segment? What is the competition like in each segment? Is the segment growing or contracting?)	. . . .	. . . .	. . . .

3. Product/Service
List (in order of priority) the features you will be providing for each segment.   . . . .

4. Benefits
List (in order of priority) the principal benefits each segment will get from using your service or product.   . . . .

5. Price
Write down your price. Can you offer different prices to each segment? (There is more on pricing in Chapter 6 – read this before you make a final decision on price.)   . . . .

6. Promotion
Write down your main promotional method for each segment (e.g. newspaper advertising, direct mail, telesales, and so on). Promotion is discussed in detail in Chapter 10.   . . . .

7. Place
Place is discussed in detail in Chapter 4.   . . . .

Checklist

- Have you segmented your market? That is, broken your market into logical segments that are different from each other?

- Are there enough people in each segment for you to sell to?

- What percentage of your business will you get from each segment? Which is the most profitable? (It can be a mistake to load yourself with low profit, high volume work. Concentrate on what will really bring the money in.)

- Are your features linked to what the customers in each segment want? Are these features ranked in order of importance?

- Can you define the principal benefits required by your customers in each segment? Can you rank them in order of importance?

- Have you considered relating your pricing to each segment? Will some segments pay you more for your goods and services than others?

- Remember to consider the remainder of your Ps – Promotion, Place and also People, Process and Physical Evidence.

■ **Marketing research**

Entering a market always involves a certain amount of risk. It's therefore essential to check whether you can meet your sales and profit objectives from the market segment/s you have chosen to target.

If you carry out an exercise like the one above, when you do your marketing research you will have formulated your own ideas to the point where you will be in a position to establish whether your gut instinct about your business ideas are correct or not. You will then need to think about everything you have in mind in relation to what the market and your competitors are already doing. This may mean that you have to choose another segment, or adapt your ideas to bring you in line with what your customers want or help you differentiate yourself from the competition.

Your segmentation grid will now begin to look like the one shown on the opposite page.

But remember: don't set your heart on it. Bear in mind that you may have to choose a different segment.

	Segment 1	Segment 2	Segment 3
1. Name your segment/s Competition are in:	. . . .	. . . .	. . . .
2. Percentage of business Competition have:	. . . .	. . . .	. . . .
3. Product/service features Competition are giving:	. . . .	. . . .	. . . .
4. Benefits Competition are saying:	. . . .	. . . .	. . . .
5. Price Competition are charging:	. . . .	. . . .	. . . .
6. Promotion Competition are doing:	. . . .	. . . .	. . . .
7. Place Competition are doing:	. . . .	. . . .	. . . .

EXAMPLE

Jim wanted to be a landscape gardener. When he went into business he found there was too much competition. He then realized that what people wanted was someone to cut lawns. So he changed his name to 'Lawn Cutting Services' and found he could make a good living.

When you think up an idea, make sure you write down all the ways in which it could make a living for you. Then see what your customers want. Don't just do what you want to do. Adjusting to the market can be a frustrating process but it's vital if you want to succeed in business. For some people, however, it just isn't possible.

EXAMPLE

Joseph was a very talented and creative artist. His pictures were exciting, vivid and had a great sense of passion. Sadly, they did not appeal to the mass market and he was driven to finding another source of income. He toyed with the idea of book illustration, but he couldn't get used to the idea of having to tailor his work to fit somebody else's imagination. In the end, rather than having to compromise his artistic integrity, he chose to work part-time in a bar. He could still paint in his spare time.

There are many ways to segment a market. Some of the ways will give you a clear picture of who your customers are and some won't tell you anything. To be any use at all, segments should give you some idea of the size of your market. They should also help you work out how to reach your customers (e.g. what papers they read, and where they live). Armed with this information, you should be able to design a product/service which you can sell to those segments profitably.

3 How to check your idea

You now need to check whether your idea will work in practice or whether you need to change it. Marketing research is the name given to this process of checking whether your business idea is really viable.

Information

Managing a business means managing information and there is usually either too much information about or not enough of it. This can be very confusing, especially if you're not sure at first what information you need. Essentially, you are looking for information that will help you reduce the risk of failure and will enable you to make safer business decisions both now and in the future. You will need to persevere; information is often there but can be difficult to locate. You'll also have to weigh up the benefits against the costs of getting a piece of information. Information in itself is worth nothing, but it could be of tremendous value if it prevents you from making a very expensive mistake in which you lose all your money.

Many people will find this information-gathering process difficult, for various reasons: they have not formulated their own ideas in the first place and so they don't know what they are looking for; or the information they need is difficult to find and hard to make sense of. And then there are some people who would rather not know – the energy used to create a business develops its own momentum; it somehow makes people rush into creating a business without thinking about it enough first.

■ Needs, wants and demands

The first step is to clarify the difference between your customers' needs, wants and demands. Needs can be physical and social. They are not created; they exist as part of our human makeup. For example, food is a basic need. Wants, on the other hand, are human needs that have been shaped by culture and individual personality. For example, in the food market, your tastes will be shaped by your personality and your culture. For all sorts of reasons, you may prefer to buy a hamburger rather than eat in an Italian restaurant.

People have unlimited wants but limited money. This means they have to choose the products that give them the most satisfaction for their money. When backed by buying power, wants become demands.

When you are doing your research be careful that you are not assessing wants. It is only when you know that people will be prepared to put their hands in their pockets and pay for your goods or services that you can be sure there is a real demand.

■ Product choice set

Product and services also compete with each other. They do this directly and indirectly. The product choice set is the range of products/services people choose from when they make a purchasing decision. For example, a new hairstyle can compete indirectly with a person's decision to buy a new dress, attend an exercise class or try out a new scent. They can also compete directly when the actual choice is being made. For example, when the person has to choose a product from a display of similar products.

When you are checking your ideas and assessing their potential, needs, wants, demands and product choice set are important factors to consider.

Market intelligence

Market intelligence refers to the process of collecting information about the market that will help you to assess and develop your ideas. You can get it from a very wide variety of sources: by just listening to what people say about competitors; by reading business publications; by watching what competitors do; by going to trade fairs, by talking to informed people in trade associations; by talking to advertising agencies, shops and wholesalers and so on. Intelligence gathering means finding out everything you can about your competitors. It is not a time to take the moral high ground.

Market research

Market intelligence may not be able to give you all the detailed information you need. In this case you will need to carry out some market research. This will mean defining your problem very clearly and formulating your research objectives. This is often the hardest step.

Once you have decided on your research objectives, you can start gathering data. The data falls into two categories: secondary data, which is information that exists and has already been collected for another purpose (you will have come across this sort of data while you were doing your market intelligence work); and primary data, which is the data that you will collect for the specific purpose of meeting your research objectives.

This is an area on which you can end up wasting a lot of time if you're not careful. It is very easy to collect useless information. For this reason, if you're intending to carry out any large-scale research, it's best to get some professional help with your questionnaire and sampling methods, as the way in which a question is asked can have a great influence on the answer you get back. Marketing or market research firms should be able to help but make sure you can afford their fees before you call them in.

How to do it
The extent and type of market research you do will very much depend on the type of business you're going into. You need to check your ideas in three ways:

1. Analyse the market.

2. Analyse your competitors.

3. Test your idea.

1. Analyse the market

Businesses are not islands cut off from what is happening in the rest of the world. Political events, governments, overseas competition, the position of suppliers, the price and availability of labour, transport, social attitudes and the general state of the economy can all affect businesses. Businesses of similar types make up a market (such as a vegetable or meat market). These markets can increase or decrease in value. If a market is decreasing, it generally means that some of the people running small businesses will be losing money. Before you start a business you must find out what is happening in the market that could affect you. For example, if the housing market goes down, and there is no government investment in social housing, there will be a general slump in the building market. This will then affect builders, carpenters, plumbers, surveyors, architects, estate agents and everyone else involved in selling and fitting out houses.

You can get this type of information by reading reports and articles in newspapers and magazines. There will also be specific information which covers different markets. Look at the list of sources of information in this chapter (see p. 43) and use your local library. Decide what you need to find out to give you a general feel for the market and telephone or visit people who know about the type of business you're going into. Don't take advice from willing amateurs. People who are informed will be found in trade associations, councils, committees and boards, hobby clubs and societies, public relations and advertising agencies.

If you're going to be working locally, once you have found out what is happening at a national level you could start trying to uncover what is happening in your own area. You can do this by speaking to your local Enterprise Agency, Council, Training and Enterprise Council, Business Clubs and the Chamber of Commerce (see Useful addresses). Check if there are any local laws that can stop you doing what you plan to do.

2. *Analyse your competitors*

When you have analysed the market and identified your customers you will be able to establish who your competitors are. Locate the right directory in a public or business library or look in the *Yellow Pages*. You can also write to the relevant Trade Association (see Useful addresses) and ask for a list of their members.

Once you have found out who your competitors are, you can start researching their marketing mix (the 4Ps or 7Ps). When you know how they have designed their marketing mix you will be able to design a mix of your own that will distinguish you from them and enable you to produce the kind of response you want from your target market.

- Product
  When you design your product you must think about: features, options, quality, style, brand name, packaging, sizes, services, warranties, returns.

- Price
  When you price your product/service you must think about:
  list price, discounts, trade-in allowances, payment period, credit terms.

- Place
  When you place your product you must think about: channels, coverage, locations, inventory, transport.

- Promotion
  When you promote your product or service you must think about:
  corporate image, advertising, personal selling, sales promotion, publicity.

For services you'll need to add another 3Ps:

- People (anyone in contact with customers, even the customers themselves).

- Physical Evidence (the actual physical objects used in providing the service and the atmosphere they create).

- Process (how the service is delivered – the sequence, capacity and its quality control).

In the beginning the only person involved will be you, but if you start employing others you will need to pay special attention to the interaction between your staff and your customers.

You will also need to consider whether the customers buying from you will be different from those actually using your product/service. This could have a major effect on the way you design your promotion.

EXAMPLE: A TOY
user: child
influencer: child's friends
decider: parents
buyer: one or both parents

EXAMPLE: A PHOTOCOPIER
user: typist, general office staff
influencer: department head
decider: purchasing committee
buyer: buying department
gatekeeper: receptionist

Having obtained the names and addresses of your competitors, you can write to them to obtain information. If you need to check their prices you can ask them to cost a job for you. You will need to look at their sales literature to see what they are saying about themselves and their letterhead to see how they are presenting themselves.

Analyse the strengths and weaknesses of their marketing mix. If they are better than you, work out a way to overcome your weaknesses. If they are weaker than you, take advantage of their weaknesses as they will be doing of your weak points.

You could also ask your competitors for help. You may be appalled by this idea, but it could be a very wise move. You may not want to ask anyone in your immediate area, but you could ask your local Enterprise Agency for an introduction to someone in the same line of business in another area. They could help you develop your marketing mix and give you advice on costs and any pitfalls. Larger companies are also a potential source of help; they may not see you as a danger and may therefore be willing to help you in all sorts of ways. Ask: they can only say no and if you don't ask, you don't get.

What to find out from your competitors

How do their customers buy from them? For example, do they buy a 'one off', do they need a sample, a trial or do they buy on impulse?

How do their customers pay? For example, is it by cash, credit or credit card? If it's credit, how long do they take to pay?

When do people buy from the competition? For example, what time of day, day of the week, time of year? Are there any seasonal fluctuations? Is there any way you could sell more by extending the times at which purchases can be made? By opening in the evening perhaps? Will it be profitable? How long will people take to get used to the idea before they buy from you?

What is the size of purchase? For example, how much do customers buy from the competition, how often do they purchase and what is the size and value of their average purchase? You will need to consider these in relation to your sales estimate and whether you could produce this quantity. Will you have enough working capital to fund it?

What methods do your competitors use to promote themselves? If possible, find out how much money they spend and when they spent it. Analyse what your competitors say about themselves in their promotional literature. Are they expressing themselves well or could they be giving people a different message? Is there anything they should be saying about themselves that they aren't? Can you take advantage of anything they are not doing? What do your competitors' customers and middlemen think of their promotional material? What is wrong with it?

If your competitors employ salespeople, find out how many they have, how often they call, whether their customers are satisfied with their methods of selling and what sales aids they use. What after-sales service are your competitors giving? How do they deal with incorrect invoices, wrong or short delivery, repairs, servicing, out-of-date or broken goods, complaints, installation, training, provision of parts and guarantees? You'll need to be *very* tactful when you ask this sort of question.

Where do your competitors sell from: wholesaler, home, market stall, vehicle, door to door, party plan (for example, tupperware), factory, own shop, exhibitions, direct mail, direct advertising, telephone, speciality shops (for example, jewellers, boutiques, etc.)? Are there any places the competition could be selling from that they aren't using? Can you take advantage of their weaknesses? What attitude do the middlemen have towards the competition? How much stock do they carry? What other aspects could be important: methods of ordering, delivery times, delivery service, methods of transport, pallet size, pricing structure, discounts, promotion?

3. Test your idea

Once you know what is happening in the market and what your competitors are up to, you should have a better idea of what you need to find out from your potential customers. You will then have to think about your research objectives and decide what questions to ask. In addition you will need to consider:

- Which method to use.

- How to ask the questions.

- Who to ask.

- How many people to ask.

Which method will you use?

If you are working alone and only have a small amount of money to spend, it's best to use a combination of mail and telephone. It will make things easier if you try and formulate a questionnaire. Test it out to see if it works. Don't ask questions unless the answers are going to confirm or change what you intend to do. You want answers that will help you make better decisions. You may want to use a tape-recorder.

You can also carry out your research face to face – you're probably familiar with the sight of people on street corners or knocking at doors doing this sort of research. If you decide to use this method you will need to write a questionnaire. This may sound easy but writing a good questionnaire can be quite tricky and you may need some help from a market research or marketing firm.

You can also get very good results by getting a number of people together in a room and having a group discussion. For example, if you had a name for your company and wanted to check whether or not people thought it sounded appealing, you could get a group of your potential customers together and ask them what they thought.

How will you ask the questions?
You need to think about how you will ask the questions, as they can be phrased in different ways to get different responses:

1. A closed question where the answer could only be 'Yes'/'No'/ 'Don't know'. For example: 'Do you like. . . ?'

2. An open question designed to encourage people to explain how they feel and think. For example: 'How does it make you feel?' or 'What does it make you think of?' 'What is your opinion about. . . ?' The aim is to get them talking so that you can really find out what they think and feel.

3. A multi-choice question where a series of set answers are given and one is chosen. For example: 'If you went out to eat, which type of restaurant would be your first choice – English, French, Italian, Indian, Chinese?'

4. A direct question where you ask a question relating to the person's behaviour. For example: 'Do you buy. . . ?' or 'Do you watch. . . ?'

5. An indirect question where you ask people what they think other people do. In this way the respondents' own attitudes may be revealed.

How to use a combination of mail and telephone
Stage One: Find out the name of the person you wish to speak to and write a short note explaining what you're trying to do and enclosing your questionnaire.

EXAMPLE
1. Do you purchase _____? YES/NO
  If NO go to question 5.
  If YES go to question 2.

2. How many _____ do you buy in twelve months?
   What type? _____
   Which supplier do you use? _____

3. Are you satisfied with your present source in terms of:
   delivery time _____ because _____
   price _____ because _____
   quantity discount _____ because

   _____

   reliability of supply _____ because

   _____

4. Would you be prepared to consider another supplier?
   YES/NO/MAYBE
   If NO please explain why: _____
   If YES please explain why: _____
   If MAYBE please explain why: _____

5. Are you likely to purchase in the next one year/two years/three
   years?   YES/NO/MAYBE

Thank you for your help. I appreciate the time you have given to
this research. I will telephone you in a week and take down your
reply.

Stage Two: Make sure that you telephone the person back in a
week.

How many people will you ask?
It is always difficult to know how many people you should ask. The
aim is to get enough replies to give you a clear indication of the
direction you should take in your decision-making. This may mean
going to a few people, and if they all say the same thing, and if you
think they are truly representative, you need go no further; or it
may mean going to more. How many you go to will depend on the
information you want. If you want to get explanations and reasons
why, choose a few people and spend a longer time with them. If
you want to get information to help you estimate the quantity you
can sell, then you will have to speak to more people. Always
choose people who you think are in the group most likely to buy
from you.

Having this information will give you power and authority. Research is not some abstract idea; it is a process you must go through in order to know your market, find out whether your idea is viable, see how you compare with the competition and discover whether you need to adapt your original idea. Without some exploration of this sort, you risk failure. And you could miss out on some great opportunities!

Test the market

It is always possible to test your business idea out on a small scale to see if it really works and then make changes based on the feedback you get from the market.

■ Sources of information
To contact any of the organisations listed below, check the details given in 'Useful addresses' (p. 172).

- Your local Enterprise Agency and Training and Enterprise Council should be able to help you with your market research.

- The following publications can generally be found in a good public library.
  They are sold by HMSO and the Central Statistical Office:
  Guide to Official Statistics
  Annual Abstract of Statistics
  Social Trends
  Business Monitor SDO 25 Retailing
  Census of Population
  Key Statistics for Urban Areas
  County Reports

- Companies House holds copies of the annual report and accounts of every limited company.

- Industrial Training Boards have information on their markets and have various publications for sale.

- Mintel Publications publish reports on different markets. You can purchase these direct from Mintel or read them at the Science Library or the business libraries of universities.

- Euromonitor Publications publish reports on different markets. You can purchase these direct from Euromonitor or read them at the Science Library or the business libraries of universities.

- The *Marketing Pocket Book* (published by the Advertising Association in association with NTC Publications).

- The Chamber of Commerce will give important information on your local business scene.

- The Institute of Marketing.

- The Association for Information Management.

- Your local library.

- The Department of Trade Library.

- The following directories should be available in a public or business library:
  Yellow Pages
  Thomson's Directory
  Directory of British Associations
  Directory of Councils, Committees and Boards
  Kompass
  Kelly's

■■■■■■■ Internal records

You will not have any internal records when you start but, once you get going, you'll be able to generate a lot of information by keeping careful records (e.g. of who buys your product and when). This, together with the information you get from the external environment, will provide a sound basis for the way you run your business and one you can use to help with any future marketing decisions.

Marketing

Once you have gathered together all the information from your market research you will have to start trying to make sense of it. It may be helpful to analyse the information in a more formal manner by doing a SWOT (short for Strengths, Weaknesses, Opportunities and Threats). This means looking at your internal strengths and weaknesses and then looking at the external opportunities and threats.

■ **Strengths, Weaknesses, Opportunities and Threats (SWOT)**
An example of a SWOT is given below. Look at each item and relate it to your own business idea.

Internal assessment
Think about your strengths and then your weaknesses. Once you have done this, think about what you have to do to overcome the weaknesses.

	Strengths	*Weaknesses*	*Action*
Marketing mix			
product/service			
pricing			
place			
promotion			
advertising			
public relations			
sales promotion			
selling			
corporate image			
people			
process			
physical evidence			
Allocation of resources			
Finance			
Plant and equipment			
Employees/management			

External assessment

Think about all the opportunities and threats facing you. Once you have done this, think about what you must do to overcome the threats and take advantage of the opportunities.

	Opportunities	*Threats*	*Action*
UK government			
UK economy			
Social trends			
Suppliers			
Overseas			
Technology			
Market			
Competition			

Having done your swot, you should have a clear idea of what you need to do in order to overcome your weaknesses, develop your strengths and take advantage of any opportunities in the external environment, while at the same time being aware of any threats you might have to face. You will now be in a position to develop your marketing strategy.

Summary

In order to analyse the opportunities in the market you need information about customers and how they make buying decisions, competitors, suppliers, re-sellers and anybody else your business will have contact with.

In addition, you need to know about environmental factors that will affect your business and your customers, such as changes in the social structure, the economy, technology, politics, imports, overseas markets, and suppliers.

This information can be gained through internal records, published information and your own questionnaires.

No company can satisfy everybody so you need to choose which group of customers you can serve most profitably and better than your competitors. You must therefore:

- Make a careful estimate of the current and future size of the market and its various segments.

- Identify all competing products, estimate their current sales and determine whether the market is large enough.

- Think about the future growth of the market. (Potential for growth may depend on the growth rate of a certain segment such as age, income, or a nationality group that uses the product more. It can also be related to changes in the environment, economic conditions, crime rate, lifestyle changes, etc.)

- Segment your market and position yourself in it.

There are four steps in the marketing research process:

1. Define your research objectives. They might be:

- Exploratory – to gather preliminary information that will help define the problem and suggest aspects that need to be investigated.

- Descriptive – describing such factors as market potential, demographics, attitudes, etc.

- Causal – to test hypotheses such as cause and effect. For example, if we put the price of this book up would people still purchase it?

When you're carrying out your research you may start off with one objective which then leads to others.

2. Develop the research plan.
The second step requires you to identify the information needed and develop a plan for gathering it.

Information is classed as secondary and primary. Secondary information exists elsewhere and can come from internal or external sources, including: internal records; government publications; periodicals and books; or commercial data.

Some of the problems you may come across with secondary information are that:

- It may not exist.

- It may be unusable.

- It may not be relevant.

- It may not be accurate; sometimes it has not been reliably collected and reported.

- It may not be up-to-date.

- It may not be impartial; sometimes it is not objectively collected and reported.

Primary information is gathered for a specific purpose. You can get this type of information by: looking at what people are doing; carrying out a survey; or carrying out an experiment.

You can use a number of different methods to collect primary information, including: telephone; personal interviews; or a combination.

Work out a sampling plan, covering: who is to be surveyed; how many people you need in your sample; and how you will proceed.

3. Put the research plan into action.

4. Interpret the findings and present them in your business plan.

4 *Finding premises*

When you start your own business you'll have to find somewhere
to work. The place you choose will very much depend on the type
of business you're starting and this will depend on whether you
manufacture goods, sell them or offer a service. The place
(building, type of outlet and location), as one of the Ps in your
marketing mix, will form an integral part of your business plan
and, in the case of a shop, hotel or restaurant, this decision can
make or break the business.

Very frequently people who are starting a business make two
mistakes. Firstly, they don't give enough thought to the place as a
part of their marketing mix, or they put too much importance on it
and get premises that are more prestigious and expensive than they
really need. They do this partly because they need to feel good
about themselves and partly because they believe the address will
give people a clear statement about how successful they're going to
be. This may well be true, but do be careful not to burden
yourself with heavy overheads before you have even started.
Remember that your business may take time to get established and
there are other aspects which may be even more important. For
example, punctuality, politeness, general neatness, tidiness, clean-
liness and a sense of order may be more important to potential
customers than a luxurious office full of expensive furniture.

Before you get a place make quite sure that you will make enough
money to pay for it and don't sign a lease before you have spoken

to a solicitor, checked with the planning department, completed your business plan, raised the money and had the building surveyed.

If you can afford it and think that you're going to be in the same place for some time you may want to think about buying your premises as this could provide more security in the long term. However, it may be wiser not to tie up all your money in this way. Then again, in some businesses, such as hotels and guest houses, it is more usual to buy them.

▬▬▬▬▬▬ Finding the right place

Do think about your customers first. Although your premises may be handy for you to get to work, if they are in the wrong place you won't get enough customers. With a retail shop, location is the most important thing to consider. Planning permission may be required if you are changing the use of the premises. This can take a very long time, especially if there is any disagreement, and if the decision is unfavourable you may have to look elsewhere. Changes to the structure and external signs will have to be discussed with the planners as well. Take your time over this because if you don't approach the Council carefully it can be difficult, or even impossible, to straighten things out once the planning committee get involved.

You can get advice about the availability of premises from estate agents, local papers, the Council and your local Enterprise Agency. The Enterprise Agency will give you advice on any special deals you can get. When you rent premises, you will have to sign a lease that will commit you to renting the property for a particular length of time; it will also have certain conditions (which may be negotiable). Before you sign anything, get a solicitor to explain it all to you. It is also a good idea to talk to a local chartered surveyor.

Business space is charged by the square foot, so you must work out how much space you need. Allow room for desks, filing cabinets, work benches, machinery, storage (materials and finished goods). Also think about lighting, toilets, heating, power-points, rubbish, locks, fire extinguishers and the closing time of the premises. And if you are employing other people remember to allow space for them as well. The law says you must provide a specific amount of space for each person. Check all this with your local Health and Safety Officer.

Working from home

If at all possible, try to start by working from home. The benefits are obvious: no rent or overheads. You can also claim a proportion of the expenses of running your home as a business. However you should discuss this with your accountant, as the benefits need to be weighed up against the cost of paying capital gains tax when you sell the house. You won't have to waste time and money travelling to work and this will add hours to your day. The problem may then be one of never being able to stop working because there is always something else to do!

However you must find out from the planning department at your local Council if there are any restrictions on working from home, as these will change from area to area in line with different classes of use. If you live in rented accommodation it may well be a breach of your tenancy agreement to run any sort of business from your home. If you have a mortgage your building society may not like it either. Be very discreet when you make your enquiries. Very often, in their anxiety to do everything correctly, people submit full-blown planning applications which are totally unnecessary and may even push the decision-makers into having to make a negative ruling. Tread softly and get advice from the officer in your local planning department. You should also take out additional business insurance, as your ordinary policy may not cover you for loss or damage to office equipment.

Do be careful about neighbours. If they complain about your noise or dirt, cars parked outside, excess traffic in the street or too many people calling at your home, you'll soon be made to stop. Although working at home is becoming more popular, people still want to retain the residential atmosphere of their neighbourhoods, and if you do anything to disturb this, there will inevitably be complaints. However, it is unlikely that you'll be able to work from home unless you're a craftsman working single-handed. Keep a low profile with no exterior sign-boards. Think about your family too and how their need for space and privacy will be affected. They will also have to learn that just because you're at home it does not mean you're not working.

When you become self-employed it is quite easy to become a total workaholic; it is even easier if you work from home. Your desk is always there and there is always something to do. This makes it very difficult to relax. Working from home will change your family life, and if your family resent the time you spend at your desk instead of being with them, there will be family feuds. It can also get quite lonely, so make sure that you get out and see other people for some of the day; otherwise the sense of isolation can be quite demoralizing. You will need to structure your day so that you start and finish work at fixed times. Allow yourself a number of short breaks during the day so that you stop working at specific times; this will help you to relax.

■■■■■■■■ Renting office space

If you're dealing with larger companies who will need to visit you and who you think will need to be impressed, you may need to work away from home. Some businesses start off by renting a small space in somebody else's office. You can even buy the use of a smart address for as little as one day a month. If all you need is a desk, and somewhere away from home where you can meet people, this may be a cheap way to start. You might even be able to share the costs of employing someone to take messages for you. If you expect people to visit you, you'll need to have a car parking space and the office should be near public transport.

■■■■■■■■ Cafés, restaurants and bars

If the premises are not being used for the same purpose as previously you'll have to get planning permission for change of use. You will also need to check with the local Environmental Health Department and the Fire Officer. Make sure you get the right position because fast-food outlets and cafés need a good location in a street where there are lots of people going past. A quality restaurant or bar can be located out of a main shopping area but adequate parking would then be an essential requirement. You will also need to check with the local Council if you want to sell alcohol for consumption on the premises.

Guest houses and small hotels

'Bed and Breakfast' guest houses need to be highly visible and situated on roads that carry a lot of traffic. Some Councils may have rules as to where 'Bed and Breakfasts' can be situated, so check before you buy anything. Hotels catering for the tourist trade need to be in places where there are a large number of tourists. You can get more information on these types of premises from your local Tourist Board. It is important to do your research carefully so that you know where they are coming from, at what times of year, what they want and whether the market is increasing or decreasing. Hotels and guest houses need to know exactly who their customers are going to be because they are catering for people on a very intimate basis.

You also need to be careful about planning permission. It can be difficult to get things changed if you take on a building in a conservation area or if it is a listed building. You will need to check with the Environmental Health Department and the Fire Officer. If you're converting a house you'll need to talk to the planning department as well. Don't sign anything before you have a survey done.

Workshops or small factories

It can be difficult to find small workshop or factory premises to start off in. The Enterprise Agency and local Councils are probably the best places to begin your search, as they will be able to tell you where to get a starter unit. Start off small and make sure your lease is flexible enough to allow you to move on without paying any financial penalties. Make sure you take advantage of any government perks for new small businesses such as free rent, reduced rates, etc. Contact your local Health and Safety Officer and find out what aspects of the law you need to comply with.

Shops

If you're going into retail the most important decision you'll have to make is the location of your shop. There is an old joke: 'What are the three most important factors to consider when looking for retail premises?' Answer: 'Location, location, location.'

How can you be sure that it's the right place? By talking to people and visiting the site on different days of the week and at different times of day. Count the number of people walking past the door and notice what they are doing. Are they carrying shopping or just walking past? Do some market research. (See Chapter 3 for information on how to design a questionnaire.) Check that there is parking and that there is reasonably easy access to the site for delivery of stock.

Good shop sites can be difficult to find and you may have to pay a higher price to get one. Don't be taken in by smart sales talk from the developers about how many people will be coming into the site. Shopping habits are changing very rapidly and what seemed a safe bet a few years ago may not be now. Do your research and do it carefully; otherwise you could lose your money.

Distribution

If you don't want your own shop and you have a product that needs to be widely distributed you'll have to sell it from more than one place. Depending on the route you take, you may have to go through a series of middlemen. These could include a processor, a wholesaler and a retailer, or a combination of all of these.

Middlemen need to make a profit as well, so your price must be high enough to give you a profit, and low enough for the middlemen to add their mark-up. At the same time, your goods must be priced so that enough people will want to buy them. This is a difficult balance to find. Do your calculations carefully.

You can also, of course, sell directly to your customers if you feel that the middlemen are putting too high a mark-up on your goods, and you think your goods will sell that way. However if you take this route it's vital to include the cost of postage, packing and delivery in your calculations. You should also consider the time and effort involved in dealing with your own distribution.

EXAMPLE
Sarah had started her business because she enjoyed sewing. She made a range of dresses that she sold mainly through craft fairs. The turnover was not high enough to make a decent living so she thought she would try selling through other outlets. When she started using middlemen her salary decreased to the point where she could barely pay her household expenses. She also had to spend much more of her time visiting these middlemen, as they needed to be encouraged to sell. They expected her, or a representative from her business, to call on them regularly to ensure that they had enough stock and to talk to them about her product. She was caught in a classic dilemma: she could take the risk of employing people to sell for her and sew her dresses for her in the hope of long-term success; she could sell direct to her target market by investing in a brochure; or she could go back to selling at craft shows, knowing that she was unlikely to increase her salary beyond the bare minimum.

The extra sales you intend to make may not be large enough to cover the extra costs involved in setting your service up. Transport, storage, promotion, administration and material costs will increase and you will need extra working capital to pay for all this. Look at your cash flow and talk to your accountant and bank manager. It is essential to get your financing right because it is very easy to get the orders and then run out of money while you are producing the goods. You can find out more about selling through middlemen on page 140.

■ **Non-store retailing**
This is a well-established and increasingly popular method of selling. It covers three types of non-store retailing: direct marketing (direct mail and mail-order catalogue), direct selling (door-to-door, party plan, a van), direct response marketing (telemarketing and direct response advertising) and automatic vending. (You can find out more direct marketing in Chapter 10.)

■ Direct selling

Door-to-Door

Door-to-Door selling used to be very popular but, as more women now go out to work, fewer people can be found at home during the day. However there are still some areas where people are at home during the day and door-to-door selling is used to sell a wide range of products and services, from knife sharpening, gardening, car and window cleaning, to cosmetics, cleaning products, insurance and double glazing. Some people enjoy doing it and organize other people to do a lot of the legwork for them. It takes patience and perseverance and can get very tiring. You also encounter a fair number of rejections, which can be difficult to cope with.

Party plan

This involves using other people's houses to sell in, which requires a bit of courage as you have to get introductions to friends of friends. Begin by asking your immediate friends if they would ask a few people round for tea. You then have a captive audience in an unthreatening environment to whom you can try and sell your product or service. The person providing the house is generally given a percentage of the takings and/or some of the product.

A Van

A van is only suitable for certain types of business. Your intial costs will be quite high, and competition can be quite fierce, especially if you are in the food business. However you may find that this is a relatively safe way to start, since if business is bad you can always move on and find a better place to trade from. The local Council will have laws and restrictions on where vans can park – so find out what the rules are before you start.

Market and Street Trading

Every area has its own laws on street trading, so make sure you talk to your local Council. You may find there are some areas you will not be allowed to trade from. You will also have to find out about the payment required for a stall and any Health and Safety regulations. Get third party insurance to protect you against any claims for damages, as you will be in a public area.

When you move in . . .

When you take over any premises remember to tell the local Council and the Post Office straight away. You should also contact British Telecom as soon as the agreements are signed, as you will need to have a telephone put in. The business rate is different from the private rate, but you will get a free entry in both the *Yellow Pages* and the ordinary telephone directory. Find out how much it costs to have your entries put in larger type – it might be well worth paying a little extra for this. Remember to get gas and electricity meters read the day you move in.

5 Making it legal

Ask a solicitor

Right from the start, you need to think about the law and how it will affect you and your business. You will have to become familiar with such terms as contracts, negligence, occupier's liability, employer's liability, product liablity, breaches of statutory duty and also criminal liability for breaches of statutory regulations. Most courses on running your own business usually cover the legal aspects. Ask your local Training and Enterprise Council for details of courses near where you live.

You will need to consult a solicitor for specific advice. However professional advice is expensive, and you can save time and money by doing as much as you can yourself, working out your ideas clearly on paper and showing them to your solicitor. Always keep your professional advisers fully in the picture and up-to-date with developments. Your local Enterprise Agency or Training and Enterprise Council may be able to arrange an initial interview with a solicitor free of charge. Your Trade Association (see Useful addresses) may also be able to help with legal advice.

The first item to discuss with any professional adviser is how much they propose to charge, and when they send out their bills. Always ask for written confirmation of these terms before instructing anyone to do any work for you. You could also consider buying a legal expenses insurance policy to cover legal fees in actions affecting your business in the future (consult your insurance adviser about this).

Legal status

What is the most appropriate legal status for your business? You could operate on your own as a sole trader, or trade with someone else as a partnership. You could form your own private company, either by yourself (with one other nominal shareholder) or with other business associates. Or you and your associates might want to form a co-operative.

Some people assume that they have to form a limited company but this is not necessarily true and you should consider a number of factors, including the different tax liabilities for different forms of business. Always consult a solicitor and an accountant about the advantages and disadvantages for your particular type of business before making a decision. If you want to form a co-operative consult your local Co-operative Development Agency.

You must be able to recognize the legal status of any business you trade with. This could be crucial, as discussed in Chapter 12 in the section on credit control.

■ Sole trader

Most people start off as 'sole traders', as this is the simplest form of business and gives you complete freedom to run your own business. All you need do is notify the Inland Revenue of your change in status to a self-employed person. Remember to send your P45 to the Department of Social Security (DSS) if you've been employed previously.

There are, however, some disadvantages in being a sole trader. Firstly, if your business fails you will be personally liable for all debts and other legal liabilities, so you might lose your home, savings and personal belongings as well as your business; and if you become unemployed you can only claim income support, not unemployment benefit.

Secondly, if your profits are high in your first year you might end up paying a high rate of tax in subsequent years, so do make provision for this. Tax on profits from a good year may have to be paid in a bad one and if you haven't set the money aside things could get quite difficult.

Many people start off as sole traders and, as the business gets bigger, they go for limited company status. The reasons are as follows: they want the protection given by limited liability; it can be easier to borrow money; and sometimes it is easier to do business with people in larger companies since they are more likely to perceive you as 'one of them'. Investors also prefer to deal with a legal entity rather than an individual.

■ **Partnership**

Finding a business partner can be likened to getting married – and it can be just as difficult! There are different ways of working with other people and you need to look honestly at your reasons for wanting to create a permanent business relationship with someone, without glossing over any potential problems. If you need extra help to develop your business it is often better to buy-in skills from other businesses when you need them. You could also employ staff but this will add to your legal responsibilities. The number of partners is limited to 20 unless you are a member of a particular profession.

As with sole traders, you must inform the Inland Revenue and the Department of Social Security. Profit is divided equally between the partners unless the partnership agreement says otherwise. Partners generally have unlimited liability, although there is statutory provision for some partners to have limited liability. Each partner is also the agent of the others, which means they are liable for contracts entered into by any other partner. And if a partner doesn't pay their income tax the Inland Revenue can sue the other partners for the money.

If you get a proper partnership agreement drawn up by a solicitor this should anticipate every eventuality and could include provisions governing:

- Type of business
- Capital requirements
- Financial transactions
- Role and tasks of partners
- How long the partnership should run for
- Conditions of termination

- What action should be taken in case of a dispute
- Competitive interests
- Starting up trading in competition to the original business
- Amount of drawings and expenses
- Share of profits and losses
- Future investment in the business
- Voting rights
- Signature on cheques
- Admission of new partners
- Holiday arrangements
- Arrangements covering absences due to illness
- Valuations of each partner's share, should a partner wish to withdraw and a new partner be admitted.
- Death of a partner

. . . and anything else you think will be important.

If you don't draw up a special agreement your partnership will be governed by the Partnership Act of 1890 and this may not suit your particular circumstances. Ask your solicitor about this.

Remember to insure the lives of your partners: you may want to use the proceeds of the policy to buy out your deceased partner's share of the business.

■ **Limited company**
A limited company requires at least two members, one of whom must be a director. You will also need a company secretary who could be your accountant or your solicitor. You can buy an 'off the shelf' company for between £120 and £150 within a matter of days from any company registration agent (see Useful addresses). Make sure you buy one that has not traded and has no debts. Although it takes only days to set up a company it can take much longer to wind it up. It is also much more expensive.

When you form a limited company you're creating a separate legal personality from your own. The constitution of the company is set out in two important documents, the memorandum and the articles of association. So you must consider your own relationship with the company: do you want to be a shareholder, an employee, a director, or all three?

Limited liability (limited to the initial cost of the shares) is not likely to be much of an advantage unless your turnover is pretty substantial and you need to protect your assets. Running costs can be higher. You must have your accounts properly audited, and an annual return must be submitted to the Registrar of Companies, as all limited companies are registered at Companies House (see Useful addresses).

On the other hand, if your business fails you may be entitled to unemployment benefit, and you won't be liable for the company's debts, other than unpaid national insurance and tax. But you must avoid the trap of giving personal guarantees to creditors, and if you are a director you must not allow the company to trade while insolvent (i.e. while its liabilities exceed its assets). If this happens a director can become personally liable for the company's debts.

■ Co-operatives

Co-operatives are halfway between a partnership and a limited company. Like companies they have limited liability and pay tax on their profits, but unlike companies the business is owned by everyone who works for them. Co-operatives can distribute the profits between their members, put the profits back into the business or give them to charity or another co-operative. Decisions are made democratically and everyone has an equal voice. Members are regarded as employees and pay tax and national insurance on their wages. See Useful addresses for further information.

Business names

You do not need to register a business unless it is a limited company or a co-operative. Whether or not you decide to trademark the name, people must be able to see who owns the business. This means that the owner's name and address must be displayed on the premises and on all business stationery, including business letters, purchase orders, invoices and receipts.

The provisions of the Business Names Act 1985 are as follows:

1. Business stationery: Letterheads, orders, invoices, statements, demands and receipts must carry, in addition to the business name, the names of all the owners and the business address in Great Britain.

2. Business premises: A sign should be placed at the premises which gives the particulars of ownership. This includes the name, address within Great Britain where documents can be served, and the full name/names of the owners.

3. Disclosure: You must disclose the name and address of your business to anyone you deal with in the course of your business.

There are also particular rules for different types of business:

■ **Sole trader**
As a sole trader you can trade under your own name, showing your initials and surname. You must also give an address where people can normally contact you. If you trade under another name, you must also show your own name and initials on business stationery.

■ **Partnership**
You must show the names of each partner, and where they can normally be contacted.

■ **Limited company**
You must show your full company name with 'Limited' or 'Ltd', registered address and address where you can normally be contacted (these two may be the same), country of registration and registered number. You do not have to show the names of the directors, but if you list one you must list them all. If your company trades under another name, you must include its full corporate name on stationery.

In addition to these points you must remember:

- Not to use a misleading or offensive name for your business.

- Not to include words such as Limited (unless you are).

- Other words, such as International, European, Royal, Bank, Scottish, Irish, Welsh, etc., need permission. Contact the Companies Registration Office (see Useful addresses).

- If you're VAT registered your VAT number must go on all your stationery.

Ask Companies House (see Useful addresses) for explanatory notes on business names and business ownership. Failure to comply with these requirements is a criminal offence. In addition a business that fails to display details of ownership may find that it is unable to enforce contracts.

■ Tax and national insurance

■ Sole traders and partnerships
Sole traders and partnerships are allowed to submit unaudited financial accounts to the Inland Revenue, but having an accountant to prepare them may save you money in the long run because your tax bill may be reduced by claiming allowable business expenses.

Sole traders and partnerships have to produce business accounts at the end of their financial year and pay tax on their profits. Depending on your personal situation, you are allowed to earn a certain amount tax-free (your personal allowance). The balance of your taxable profit is taxed according to the current rates for income tax.

Sole traders and partners must also pay national insurance and it's easiest to do this by direct debit from your bank account (you can also pay with stamps). If you earn less than a certain amount you can apply for a Small Earnings Exemption Certificate. If your profits exceed a certain figure you will pay a higher contribution related to profit. Your accountant will advise you on this.

- **Limited companies**
Limited companies are obliged to pay corporation tax on profits.

As a director of a limited company you may have to treat yourself as an employee of the company. This means that you will have to pay your income tax and national insurance through a PAYE (Pay As You Earn) system. Because you are an employee, your company may have to pay an additional sum depending on your income.

- **Employees**
If any business has employees it has to operate a PAYE scheme depending on the level of wages paid. This means that you deduct tax and national insurance and pay it to the Inland Revenue on behalf of your employees. It is usually best to get advice from an accountant on how to operate such a scheme.

- **VAT**
The rules governing VAT apply to all businesses. You must register for VAT if your business is not exempt and your turnover is likely to exceed the VAT threshold (check this figure with your local VAT office as it sometimes changes). Make sure you keep proper records from the first day, as VAT inspectors will visit from time to time and there are penalties for dealing with VAT incorrectly.

Tax and VAT are complicated subjects in which the rules are frequently altered. There is more on VAT in Chapter 6 on costing and pricing. You will need to get specific information on allowable business expenses from your local VAT office or your accountant.

Contractual liability

The following notes apply equally to all businesses, whatever status they have. Remember that we are now in the Single European Market, and European Community (EC) law applies to all businesses. Contact the Information Centre at the European Commission (see Useful addresses) for further details of the impact of EC law.

■ **Contracts**

A contract is an agreement that is recognized in law. With some exceptions, a contract doesn't have to be in writing. Indeed we all make contracts every day of our lives, and usually without even knowing we have done so. When you run a business, however, you must be on your guard and learn to recognize the contractual obligations in all your dealings.

The agreement

In particular you must ensure that an agreement covers essential points, including:

- A clear description of the product or service.

- The fee or price, when it should be paid and whether there are any penalties for late payment.

- When the delivery will be made or the service performed.

- That ownership of goods delivered will only pass to the customer after full payment has been received.

- Details of any warranties you wish to give.

Standard terms and conditions

You will soon come across the standard form of contract supplied by other businesses. Read the terms because you will be bound by them unless you negotiate changes. You may not be able to persuade a large company to alter their terms for you, but you can always shop around to find other suppliers offering more favourable terms.

A common mistake is to assume that you have to get a very lengthy and complicated contract drawn up by a solicitor. This is not always so and it is a good idea to find out how things are done in your own particular line of business. You can quite easily put clients off by asking them to sign an over-complicated document. You must use your own judgement to ensure that the customer understands your standard terms and conditions, and that you are adequately covered for any eventuality.

■ **Consumer law**

Don't forget that there is a wealth of legislation designed to protect your customers. You ought to consult your local trading standards department for preliminary advice on all the legislation that it enforces, e.g.:

- Trade Descriptions Act 1968
- Tort (Interference With Goods) Act 1977
- Sale of Goods Act 1979
- Supply of Goods and Services Act 1982
- Consumer Protection Act 1987.

Business regulation

Unless you are a member of a profession you can usually start a business without having to get a licence. Ask your trade association for advice on any specific regulations which might affect your business (see Useful addresses). The following businesses do have to be licensed and are governed by regulations:

- Providing credit and hire, including debt recovery. (Check with your local trading standards department about registration under the Consumer Credit Act 1974.)
- Driving schools.
- Employment agencies.
- Shops, pubs, clubs, and restaurants selling alcohol.
- Providing financial advice, or a related service. (Requires registration under the Financial Services Act 1986.)
- Keeping information on people on a computer and in manual systems: this may require registration under the Data Protection Act 1984. Many small businesses wrongly assume that this legislation does not apply to them. Any organization which keeps information about

living individuals on computer is generally advised to register. Ask the Data Protection Registrar for guidance (see Useful addresses).

- Other businesses may depend on local by-laws so check with your local authority.

■ Premises

As soon as you acquire business premises you must consider the following liabilities:

- Fire precautions – contact your local fire service.

- Planning permission and advertising signs – contact your local planning authority.

- Business rates – contact your local authority.

- Security – contact your local police Crime Prevention Officer.

■ Employees

Before you employ anyone ask the Department of Employment and your local Environmental Health Officer for guidance. Here are a few important statutes to be aware of:

- Shops Act 1950

- Fire Precautions Act 1971

- Health and Safety at Work Act 1974

- Employment Protection (Consolidation) Act 1978

- Health and Safety (First Aid) Regulations 1981.

■ Insurance

Insurance is vital. Think carefully about your risks and get advice from a broker who is a registered member of the British Insurance and Investment Brokers Association (see Useful addresses). If you're working from home your standard household contents insurance won't cover anything used in connection with your business, even though it's at the same address. You will need to take out an office insurance policy in the name of your business.

You should also check that your car insurance covers business use. Third party liability for all vehicles and employer's liability are compulsory.

Other types of insurance may not be compulsory but are still advisable. They include public liability, product liability, professional indemnity (in some professions this is statutory), business premises, plant and equipment stocks, consequential loss, goods in transit, fire and theft, business interruption, goods on a sub-contractor's premises, fidelity guarantee to cover dishonesty within your business, personal health, accident, sickness, pension, life insurance, etc.

■ **Protecting your business assets**

Trademarks
Trademarks distinguish goods from each other and the owner of a trademark has the sole right to use the mark on goods specified in the registration. A trademark can be a name, word or symbol, or a made-up name. Get general information from the Patent Office and specific advice from a patent agent (see Useful addresses).

Patent and registered design
If you apply for a patent or a registered design it must be something genuinely new, and you should not tell the public until the patent has been granted. Get advice from a patent agent.

Copyright
This is the right to protect artistic, literary and musical works from unauthorized use for fifty years (although this may change). It is automatic and does not have to be registered. Always make it clear that you reserve the copyright in your work. Put your name and the date on each piece of written material that you produce. You can give a copy of the material to your bank manager or solicitor, and get a dated receipt from them. Remember to get written permission from the copyright holder if you want to use copyright material (e.g. in a brochure or leaflet). You may have to pay a fee for reproducing it.

6 How to cost, price and make a sales estimate

You won't know if you have a good idea for your business until you have worked out how much it will cost, whether it will be profitable and whether you can get the money to carry it out. To do this you have to think about sales volume and prices. If you're frightened of figures, pay a professional to help you.

Costs

The first step is to distinguish between two types of costs: fixed overhead costs and variable costs (i.e. direct costs).

1. Fixed overhead costs
Before you start to price your product/service, or even produce accounts, you must know which of your business costs will have to be paid even if you don't sell anything. These are called fixed costs because they usually stay more or less the same, though some may suddenly go up (like rent) and others will go up if you don't keep a constant check on them (like the telephone). Others are dependent on your plans (like promotion). Some fixed costs are paid monthly, some quarterly and some only occasionally or yearly. You will need to add up the figures to get an annual total. Some examples are:

- Vehicle – purchase, hire purchase, lease, hire, petrol, servicing, repairs, tax, insurance.

- Stationery – design, printing, paper, envelopes, compliments slips, calling cards, record books, invoices.

- Premises – rent, rates, electricity, gas, water, insurance (such as public liability, employer's liability, product liability, plant and equipment), telephone, furniture, equipment costs (such as purchase, hire purchase, lease), repairs, cleaning, staff wages.

- Professional help – solicitor, accountant, business consultant, registration fees.

- Promotion – advertising costs (such as design, copywriting, advertising costs), signs, posters, direct mail, selling aids (such as leaflets, price lists, brochures, slides, films) and public relations costs (such as exhibitions, conferences, gifts, cards, entertainment, sponsorship, photographs).

- Market research, selling, distribution costs.

- Bank loan repayment, bank charges and interest.

2. Variable costs (i.e. direct costs)

You must then find out the actual cost of making your product or carrying out your service. These are called variable or direct costs because they will change all the time, depending on how much work you do. They will go up if you make and sell more and go down if you make and sell less. These will include raw materials and some labour costs directly related to making the goods or providing the services.

Costing, pricing and making a sales estimate

Your market will, up to a point, dictate your prices. However you must look at your price in relation to your costs, your sales estimates (your volume), your market segments, your 'image' and your marketing mix and what your competitors are charging.

There are various methods to help you determine the best price, and give you a break-even point and a desirable profit figure. These are: cost plus pricing; demand pricing (what the market will bear); and competitive pricing (what you need to charge in order to match the competition). In practice, people tend to use a combination of all three. Most first costings have to be changed.

■ **Cost plus pricing**
In cost plus pricing a certain amount of profit is added to the costs.

Method
1. Write down your average household expenses for the year and work out what you need to earn to cover them.

2. Now calculate and write down your average business expenses for the same period.

3. Work out the number of sales you will make over the year (you can base this calculation on the number of hours or days of work or number of products you can sell).

4. Add the household and business expenses together and then divide the total by the number of sales you think you'll make. The formula is:

$$\text{Daily rate} = \frac{\text{business overheads plus annual drawings}}{\text{annual productive hours}}$$

or:

$$\text{Product cost} = \frac{\text{business overheads plus annual drawings}}{\text{total product sales}}$$

5. Now add on the amount of profit required per unit, the direct costs and VAT (where appropriate), to reach a sales price.

EXAMPLE: COSTING AND PRICING – DAILY RATE
If you're providing a service you will need to calculate a price per day (in some cases it will be per hour).

How to estimate your expenses:

	£
Annual household expenses (including items like mortgage, telephone, heat, light, council tax, holidays, etc.)	10 000

Annual business expenses   5000
(including telephone, rent, rates, heat, light, advertising,
interest on bank loan, professional fees, etc.)

Your salary (drawings as a sole trader)   10 000

Total business expenses   15 000

How to estimate your sales (this business has decided on the
following breakdown of time):

Days in the year	:	365
(less selling days)	:	140
(less weekends)	:	104
(less holidays)	:	15
(less sickness)	:	5
(less training)	:	10
(less conference)	:	5
(less meetings)	:	11
Total days	:	290

Therefore $365 - 290$ days $= 75$ days for production

Production days are counted as 'work' as these are the only days
for which you will be paid and should generate sufficient income to
cover the non-productive days.

How to work out the cost per day (divide your costs by the number
of days you'll be getting paid):

$$\frac{£15\,000}{75\text{ days}}$$

Cost per day $=$ £200

How to work out your profit:

Desired profit (say 50% of cost) $=$ £100

Price per day is £200 + £100 = £300 per day (excluding VAT and
any direct material costs).

The minimum amount of money to be earned, based on 75 days'
work, is £22 500. When you calculate your break-even point (see
p. 77) you will get the minimum figure you must reach in order to
cover your costs.

Demand pricing

This is a more difficult system to use because you have to work out at the beginning what price you think will give you the best combination of volume and profit. This is done largely by trial and error and market research.

EXAMPLE

This table is an example of demand pricing and illustrates the value of forecasting sales where customers' margins and sales units need to be considered through different types of outlets. The retail selling price is £16.

| | Sales via | | | |
| | Wholesaler | Retailer | Chain store | Mail order |
	£	£	£	£
Ex works cost	5	5	5	5
Postage				1
Manufacturer's profit	2	4	1.5	5
Total	7	9	6.50	11
Customers' margin	6	6	4.50	
Total	13	15	11	11
Expected level of sales (units)	10 000	5 000	12 000	6 000
Projected profit for the manufacturer	20 000	20 000	18 000	30 000

■ Competitive pricing

If your competitors are well established it will be difficult for you, as a new small business, to charge more. If you do, the customer will have to be convinced that your quality, guarantees, etc. are much better than what is already being offered by the larger companies. It is also worth bearing in mind that if people are used to paying a certain price, and are willing to continue paying it, then it is not a good idea to lower it. Charge what the market is used to paying, particularly for specialist products or services. For instance, we don't generally buy brain surgery at a cut price (even if it is on special offer)! Also, the more you lower your prices, the more work you'll have to do – and why give money away? Choose the most profitable work and get the highest price for it, without being greedy.

If you find that the average market price is lower than your price, then you can do the following: reduce your overheads (for example, by moving to cheaper premises), buy cheaper materials, reduce your profit margin, work more hours or be more productive, look at 'bundling' your benefits in a different way, work days instead of hours, work on a retainer, look at your market segmentation again, etc. Or it may be better to find another idea.

■ **Pricing summary**
Always choose the price that will help you sell the most at the highest profit. People do not only base their buying decisions on price and, as a general rule, price is the last thing you should mention when selling. Don't make the following mistakes:

- Even if you're just starting out as a new business don't think that you should charge less – you can either do the work or you can't. Nobody need know you have just started; why tell them?

- If you've recently had a spell of unemployment you may want some sort of reassurance from people. This may lead you into offering lower prices than the going rate, or doing things for free. A desire for acceptance and a low self-image should not influence your pricing. There is nothing worse than getting a job and realizing halfway through that you could have got twice as much. It curdles the blood!

- Start off by charging what you need to cover your costs and make a reasonable profit. Do your costings properly and make a realistic estimate of sales. Don't be over-optimistic.

- 'Bundle' your product/service in different ways, so that people can decide for themselves whether to buy the 'whole bundle' of benefits, or fewer, depending on what they can afford.

- Realize that in the service business prices may not always be that important – people may just want *you* and be willing to pay for you! Quality counts.

- Find out what your competitors are charging.

- Understand about quality – the better a service or a product is, the higher the price you can charge.

- Your price must fit your corporate image – a quality image and price often go hand in hand. Remember the marketing mix. Your price must match your customers' perception of themselves – if you are setting yourself up as an upmarket service you can afford to charge more.

■ **Other pricing considerations**

- If your prices are too low, people may think the quality is poor.

- £3.99 looks a lot cheaper than £4.00. This is an old trick but it does work.

- Are you selling something that people are likely to want to spend more money on – gifts for someone else perhaps, or luxury goods?

- Have you thought of selling different versions – a cheaper one and a more expensive one?

- Can you sell the same thing at different times but price them differently?

- Can you sell the same thing but in different places at different prices?

- Are you the only supplier? If you are, you could probably charge more.

- What will you charge for and what will you give away free – training, fitting, repairs, delivery, packaging?

■ **Estimates and Quotations**

Don't confuse an estimate with a quotation. An estimate gives the approximate price. A quotation gives the fixed price and if it is agreed by both parties it is binding. A buyer will usually ask for a quotation in writing.

EXAMPLE

Dear Mr Everett

Garden gate – Quotation

Following our meeting I have pleasure in providing you with the following quotation to supply and fit garden gates to the side entrances to your house.

Quantity	Two gates
Specification	Six-foot wooden gates fitted with a bolt and a lock
Price	The total is £395 + VAT The terms are valid for 30 days
Terms	Payment is due 7 days from date of invoice

If you have any questions please don't hesitate to call me. I will telephone you in the next week.

Yours sincerely

Break-even point

When you have decided on your costs and your prices you can work out your break-even point. Finding your break-even point will tell you how much you need to sell in order to cover your costs. Your price will also relate to your volume of sales. You should try a number of prices and multiply them by what you expect to sell. This will give you some idea of the most profitable balance for your business. If you find this difficult ask your accountant to help you.

Try to keep your break-even point as low as possible. It is usually much easier to control costs than to make sales.

■ Preparing a break-even point

Situation

A business produces calculators and is able to sell what it produces. The variable costs (materials and direct labour) for producing each calculator are £10 (material £7 and direct labour £3). The selling price is £20 each. The fixed costs of running the business are £5000 per month. How many calculators need to be made and sold each month for the business to break-even?

Solution

You can prepare a break-even point in three ways by calculation, by table and by graph.

EXAMPLE: BY CALCULATION

	£
Selling price per unit	20
Less variable costs per unit	10
Contribution per unit	10 (i.e. $20 - 10 = 10$)

The formula for calculating the break-even point is:

$$\frac{\text{Total Fixed costs (£)}}{\text{Contribution per unit (£)}} = \text{Break-even point (number of units)}$$

Thus with fixed costs of £5000 per month, this business must sell:

$$\frac{£5000}{£10} = 500 \text{ calculators each month}$$

EXAMPLE: BY TABLE

Units of production	Variable costs	Fixed costs	Total cost	Total revenue	Profit (loss)
100	1000	5000	6000	2000	(4000)
200	2000	5000	7000	4000	(3000)
300	3000	5000	8000	6000	(2000)
400	4000	5000	9000	8000	(1000)
500	5000	5000	10 000	10 000	0
600	6000	5000	11 000	12 000	1000
700	7000	5000	12 000	14 000	2000

The table shows that 500 units is the break-even point. At this level of sales there is no loss or profit.

EXAMPLE: BY GRAPH

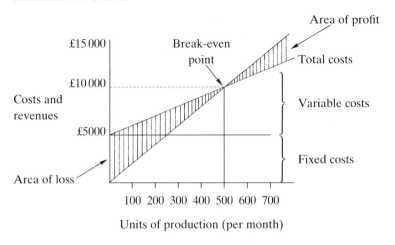

Units of production (per month)

Once again, the graph shows a break-even point of 500 units.

■ Value added tax (VAT)

VAT is an extra tax we pay to the government on certain types of goods and services. If your sales value is so high that you have to register for VAT it will mean charging your customers an extra amount to cover the payments you have to make to the government. If you deal with the general public, who are not VAT registered, you will be less competitive. However, if you are dealing with other VAT registered firms, it shouldn't make any difference.

If you don't want to register for VAT, consider getting your customers to pay for materials and hire charges themselves (possibly using your trade discount arrangement). There are three ways in which goods and services are classified:

1. Exempt supplies – no VAT is payable.
2. Zero rated – no VAT is payable on goods sold, however VAT paid on purchases can be reclaimed.
3. Standard – 17½% VAT is payable.

Ask your local Customs and Excise Office for their VAT leaflet for clarification.

If you are only dealing in exempt supplies, you do not have to pay VAT. But if you are dealing in zero or standard rated supplies, and your taxable turnover (not profit), is greater (or if you think it will get bigger), than the VAT threshold in a year, or in the next 30 days, you must register to pay VAT. Check the current threshold, as the government changes it from time to time.

Your VAT return must be filled in each quarter and you will have to complete and return your form with a cheque within 30 days from the end of the quarterly period. This includes all your invoices issued and received; even the ones you haven't been paid for, unless you're using the Cash Accounting Scheme which allows for VAT to be paid only on payments received. However you will have to get special permission from the Customs and Excise Department to do this. Small businesses with taxable sales below a certain amount can also apply for the Annual Accounting Scheme. This scheme allows you to account for your VAT by direct debit in nine monthly payments. One annual VAT return is filled in and a tenth payment is made to adjust the balance of the account.

You'll need to give proper tax invoices to other companies, showing your VAT number and amount of VAT payable. If you sell to the public you need only give a tax invoice if you're asked for one.

The VAT inspectors are very thorough and if you're a small business they may want to look at every single invoice. Talk about this to your accountant so that you can set up a system of business records that follow the VAT rules before you start. It can be difficult to change your habits later on.

■ **How to calculate VAT**
When you purchase a standard rated VAT item, you pay an extra 17½%. When you sell a standard rated VAT item, you charge your customers an extra 17½%. Because the value of your standard rated sales is usually higher than the value of your standard rated purchases you will have to pay the difference to the VAT Office. In cases where the VAT on your purchases exceeds the VAT on your sales the VAT Office will refund the difference.

SUMMARY

Input VAT is the sum you pay to suppliers on some purchases (not all your suppliers will be registered for VAT).

Output VAT is the sum you charge your customers on your sales.

How to calculate VAT

1. When the price includes VAT and you want to know the amount of VAT, multiply the prices including VAT by $\frac{17.5}{117.5}$ (not $\frac{17.5}{100}$) or multiply the price including VAT by 7 and divide by 47.

EXAMPLE

You purchase petrol for £20 including VAT.

The VAT is £20 $\times$ $\frac{17.5}{117.5}$ = £2.98

or

Using the VAT fraction

The VAT is £20 $\times$ 7 = $\frac{140}{47}$ = £2.98

2. When the price includes VAT and you want to know the original amount before VAT was added.

EXAMPLE

You purchase petrol for £20 including VAT.

The price before VAT is £20 $\times$ $\frac{100}{117.5}$ = £17.02

3. When you are a VAT registered trader.

As a VAT registered trader you buy goods worth £10 and VAT at $17\frac{1}{2}\%$ is added to the price making the bill £11.75. The £1.75 is called your input tax which you will be able to claim back. If you later sell these goods for £20 you will have to include VAT on the bill. You can work this figure out by using the fraction $\frac{17.5}{117.5}$ or $\frac{7}{47}$

(shown in example one on the previous page). The figure of £2.98 is called the output tax. When you complete your VAT return, using this one transaction as an example, you would owe £2.98 in VAT but you could reclaim £1.75, so that the net amount you would pay the VAT Office is £2.98 − £1.75 = £1.23.

If your selling price is less than your buying price, you'll get a refund. So if you're planning to buy a lot of materials and equipment, and the VAT on these purchases will be greater than the VAT you will collect back from your customers, it could be well worth registering for VAT because the VAT Office will give you a refund. This is a good idea for businesses where the extra 17½% on the price will not reduce sales because customers are VAT registered themselves and can therefore reclaim the money.

The major financial statements

You will need to prepare a cash flow forecast, a projected balance sheet and a profit and loss account. These will be included in your business plan (see Chapter 8).

■ Cash flow forecast

You may look profitable when you work out your business expenses, but don't mix up profit with cash. Profit may be money owed to you but cash is what counts most, and while you're waiting to get paid you can easily run out of cash to pay your bills.

This is a problem for new businesses because they often have to pay cash when they buy. Customers, on the other hand, want credit and take a long time to pay. Costs are also higher when you start and sales can take a long time to build up, especially if it takes about six visits to secure any business from a new customer. Your sales could also vary according to the time of year.

Expansion
If you get more orders than you anticipated and you want to expand you will need more money to meet your direct costs – more business means finding more money to carry out the work. However it can be really dangerous to expand your business faster than your cash resources can allow – many businesses go bust this way. This is called overtrading.

Emergency action in a cash crisis

Cash and profits are not the same. Profitable companies frequently go out of business simply because they run out of cash and they can't get any more money to keep them going. Here are some emergency measures you could consider in this situation:

- Stimulate cash sales with special offers and discounts in exchange for immediate cash payments.
- Sell off some of your stock of raw materials.
- Chase up overdue accounts.
- Don't buy anything unless you have to.
- Ask for credit from your suppliers.
- Take less money out of the business for yourself.
- Think about selling your premises or equipment or renting them out for cash.
- Ask your bank for another overdraft or raise more money from investors.
- Work for someone else part-time.
- Factoring.
- Use a debt-collecting service.
- Refuse or postpone orders because you'll have nothing left to pay your bills.
- Increase your prices (be sensitive to your customer's purchasing power and to competition).
- Reduce your overhead costs.
- Reduce your direct costs – materials and labour.

Preparing a cash flow forecast

The cash flow forecast is based on how you think the money will come into your business and how you think it will flow out. Instead of showing when the invoices are sent out, it shows when the actual money will change hands. It will help you determine how much financial support you will need in the form of loans, grants or overdraft facilities. Your bank will probably be able to give you a standard cash flow form or your local Enterprise Agency may be able to do one for you on their computer. A section from a sample cash flow forecast is shown on page 85.

To prepare a cash flow, you need to begin by writing the months across the top of the page, starting from when you plan to begin trading. Then divide the columns horizontally across the page into three sections:

1. Receipts/cash in: This is any money coming into the business, such as the money you're paid, money you have borrowed and money you have put in yourself, plus any other income. Show the amount in the month when it actually comes in.

2. Payments/cash out: This covers any costs incurred by the business. Show the expenses in the month they are paid. VAT is shown every quarter in the month it is paid.

3. Balances: This shows the money in your bank account at the beginning and end of each month.

If you prepare a cash flow forecast you'll be able to see where you stand from month to month. You can then take advance action and try to find out why sales are down, who hasn't paid, etc. You can often use a simple spreadsheet on a computer to do your cash flow forecast, making it very easy to update the figures each month and compare actual figures with those forecasted a few months earlier.

■ **The profit and loss account**
The profit and loss account has nothing to do with the actual money paid by your customers. It covers a fixed period (generally a year) and will tell you how much profit has been made. It also includes a figure for depreciation (20%–25%). As a sole trader you will be taxed on your profits after the fixed overheads and direct costs have been deducted.

EXAMPLE

	May		June		etc.
	Budget	*Actual*	*Budget*	*Actual*	
Sales by volume					
Sales by value					

RECEIPTS/CASH IN
Sales – cash
Sales – debts due to be paid
Capital introduced
Grants and loans
VAT

Total receipts

PAYMENTS/CASH OUT
Raw materials
Telephone/fax
Rent and council tax
Postage/carriage
Vehicle purchase
Electricity
Bank charges
Motor – fuel
Motor – Other expenses
Fees
Advertising
Drawings (your own)
Insurance
Wages and salaries and
National Insurance
Others
VAT

Total payments

BALANCES
Opening bank balance
+/− Net Position
(income–expenditure)
Closing bank balance
(carried forward to next period)

Profit and loss account for the year ended . . .

	£	£
SALES		48 270
Less direct costs (materials/labour/overheads)		33 600
Gross profit (sales − direct costs)		14 670
EXPENDITURE		
Telephone/fax	160	
Rent	3000	
Business rates	1000	
Postage/carriage	240	
Electricity	120	
Bank charges	50	
Travel	450	
Fees accountancy/consultancy	300	
Advertising	250	
Insurance	100	
Depreciation	1000	
TOTAL		6670
NET PROFIT (gross profit − total expenditure)		8000

■ **The Balance Sheet**
The balance sheet gives a snapshot of the position of the business
at a specific point in time.

	£	£	£
	cost	depreciation	net
FIXED ASSETS			
Equipment	5000	1000	4000
			4000

CURRENT ASSETS

Stock	1000	
Debtors (customers)	2000	
Cash at the bank	10 000	
	13 000	

LESS
CURRENT LIABILITIES

Loans (short-term)	2000		
Creditors	4000		
		6000	
NET CURRENT ASSETS (working capital)			7000
NET ASSETS			11 000

FINANCED BY:

Capital (opening balance)	2000		
Add profit (profit & loss account)	8000		
	10 000		
Less drawings	4000		
Capital (closing – carried forward)		6000	
Add long term loan		5000	
			11 000

The current assets less the current liabilities gives you the money or assets that can be turned into cash. This is your working capital. Note that your total should always equal the net assets.

The balance sheet shows you the total assets and total liabilities of the business at a point in time:

- The current assets of the business–money in the bank, stock, and money due from customers.
- The current liabilities-creditors (trade) and accruals (other unpaid bills).
- How solvent the business is.
- How quickly the assets can be turned into cash.
- What the fixed assets are.
- Where the money comes from.
- Is the business overtrading or undertrading.

7 How to find the money

A business can't hope to succeed unless it gets its financing right. Most people who start their own businesses are not accountants and therefore don't have the knowledge and experience that is necessary to decide on the best way to finance their business. Your accountant, bank manager or Enterprise Agency should be able to expand on the information given to you in this chapter. This is an area where people sometimes make mistakes because they are over-optimistic about how much money they will make, and how long it will take for the money to come in.

EXAMPLE

Sue ran a consultancy business and when she first started she had one very large client, for whom she had briefly worked in the past. One of the directors took a personal interest in her progress and put substantial amounts of business her way. The director then retired and she lost his company's business before she had time to find any more customers. The fatherly interest this man had taken in her had ensured that she was paid regularly and promptly.

When she ventured out into the real world, she discovered that in her type of business it took about two years, numerous telephone calls, over six visits and a free sample of her work, to build up a client's confidence sufficiently for them to give her any work. She also found that large companies cover a proportion of their working capital requirements with 'free trade credit' – which means that their suppliers give them a certain amount of time to pay for services received. She nearly went out of business because of late payments and an incorrect estimate of how long it would take to get started.

Use this information as an introduction to a complicated subject, not as a substitute for financial advice from a professionally trained accountant. You should also bear in mind that the legal structure you choose for your business – sold trader, partnership, limited company or co-operative – and the type of finance you use will have important cost and tax implications.

■ The main sources of business finance

■ Core capital

Do remember that a fair amount of money is normally permanently tied up in the business as working capital, represented by stocks and debtors (less creditors). This is the core working capital and because it is virtually permanent it should be looked upon as part of the long-term financial needs of the business. Never underestimate this.

There are three main ways of getting money: borrowing, investing or getting a grant.

■ 1. Borrowing

Borrowed money is called loan capital and it eventually has to be paid back, usually with some interest added to it. The security may take the form of a charge on a specific business asset, or a floating charge on all the assets (which means that if your business fails the lender will get their money back before any other creditors).

If your business has no assets the lender will want some form of personal security from you, such as stocks and shares, an existing life insurance policy, a term life assurance policy, a charge on your home or a guarantee from someone else. If you decide to do this you'll be putting your own security at risk. It is not something to be done unless you absolutely have to, because it removes the protection a limited liability structure would otherwise give you.

The usual course of action is to ask your bank manager for an overdraft. An overdraft is a temporary loan to tide you over between the time you have to pay your suppliers' bills and the time your customers pay you. You will have to pay interest on this money, and the payments have to be made whether or not the business is doing well. Overdrafts are repayable on demand. This means that if you are going through a bad patch, and can't find the money when it is demanded, the bank can close you down. In the beginning, most businesses spend more money than they make and if you can't finance yourself over this period you are unlikely to succeed.

Borrowed money always carries a cost, so you need to find out about fixed and variable rates of interest. You should also ask the bank about arrangement fees, early repayment fees and non-utilization fees. It's worth trying to negotiate in order to reduce the various payments. Shop around for the best terms. But it is unwise to sacrifice a good long-term relationship with your bank for the sake of a miniscule gain elsewhere.

For tax purposes, you can offset the interest on the loan or overdraft against your profits, but this is not a good idea if it means putting your business in a vulnerable position, as illustrated by the following story.

EXAMPLE
Interest rates were low when Jack took out an overdraft and invested the money in his business. He planned to deduct the interest on the borrowed money from his profits in order to improve his tax position. What he didn't realize was that the rate of interest was not fixed and the payments could go up. They did so at the same time as business went down. The bank manager was not too impressed by Jack's company and as Jack was having difficulty meeting his payments the bank manager asked for the money back: end of story!

■ **2. Investing**
You can invest in your own business or you can ask other people to invest in your idea. You will need to speak to your accountant and solicitor if you decide to follow this path.

■ **3. Getting a grant**

Grants generally have to be applied for before you set up your business, though there are some exceptions. They normally have conditions attached to them. For example, they might have to be used only to purchase equipment and not for paying wages. Find out about the conditions first. For more information on grants contact your local Council or your local Training and Enterprise Council.

■ **Combinations**

Most businesses combine the different types of finance, depending on their size. For example, you might decide to use any of the following combinations:

- Your capital + overdraft.

- Your capital + overdraft + bank loan.

- Your capital + overdraft + bank loan + grant.

- Your capital + overdraft + bank loan + grant + investor.

Look at the different types of money below and that should give you an even better idea of some of the options open to you.

Main types of finance arrangement

The most important thing to remember is to get the right type of money. Money is the life-blood of any business, and without it, will die a quick and nasty death. It is vital to recognize that there are two types of business finance: borrowed short-term money and medium/long-term money. It is also very important to remember that businesses quite often fail if they don't get the right balance between owner's money and borrowed money.

Before you go in search of money you must think about whether it is for short or long-term needs.

Short-term money (up to three years) is intended to keep you going while you are waiting to get paid, and to help buy raw materials. This is the working capital which is used to finance the current assets and its importance should never be underestimated. Examples are: bank overdrafts; short-term bank loans; bills of exchange; debt factoring and invoice discounting; hire purchase and instalment credit; and trade credit from suppliers.

Medium to long-term money should be used to buy things that will last. This is called fixed capital and is needed to finance fixed assets (such as tools, buildings, equipment and vehicles). This money is tied up for three years or more. There are two types:

1. Where the aim of the business is to own the money, these are equity capital (ordinary shares and deferred ordinary shares) or preference share capital (preferred ordinary shares and preference shares).

2. Where the aim is to borrow money or to get it from another source, you might choose any of the following medium or long-term financial arrangements: mortgages; sale and leaseback of premises; hire purchase and instalment credit; lease; credit insurance and guarantee arrangements to help small exporters; project finance or joint venture finance; medium and long-term bank loans; loan stocks and debentures; and convertible loan stocks.

■ **Short-term money**

Bank overdrafts
This is the most common form of borrowing. All you need do is speak to your local bank manager, though you'll need to write out your business plan first (see Chapter 8). Do remember that overdrafts are repayable on demand, which means that you should not use an overdraft to finance any long-term need – banks can force you to repay the money immediately if they feel worried about the way your business is going. For this reason, you should never use an overdraft to finance long-term needs.

Interest rates also vary, so don't make the mistake of borrowing a lot of money when rates are low and then being unable to pay them when they increase. Banks charge for arranging overdrafts so it is important to try and get it right first time. Once you have agreed your overdraft limit it is not a good idea to exceed it. It costs you money and does your business reputation no good.

■ **Term loans (short, medium and long)**
This is a safer way of borrowing money, although it is more expensive than an overdraft and will involve you in fees. Term loans are used to meet your permanent working capital needs and can be taken out to cover periods of up to 20 years. They must either be secured against a fixed asset or personally guaranteed by you (or another director). You will have the use of the money for the period that you agree on, unless you fail to pay the interest. Repayment terms vary and can be negotiated.

■ **Bills of exchange**
Very often a business can have customers but not enough money to finance producing its next order because it is waiting for previous customers to pay their bills. A bill of exchange is rather like a post-dated cheque which is sold to a third party for cash. It can be used to replace or supplement overdraft facilities.

■ **Debt factoring and invoice discounting**
Customers who take a very long time to pay are a problem for businesses that are growing fast – and where cash flow is a problem. This means that the money you need to expand is just not there because it is tied up in unpaid bills. This problem can be solved by debt factoring and invoice discounting. This involves getting the money your customers owe you by selling your trade debts to a factoring company. This service will cost you a little more than normal bank overdraft rates and you'll need to be reasonably established, with a turnover of more than £25 000. You can contact debt factors and invoice discounters through your accountant.

Unlike debt factoring, where all your unpaid bills are sold to the factor, in invoice discounting you need only sell certain invoices. You therefore remain in sole charge of administrating and collecting the trade debts of your business. If your debtors don't pay the invoices you have sold, you will have to pay the money back to the discount house.

■ **Hire purchase and instalment credit**
You may decide that instead of raising money to make an outright

purchase (e.g. of new equipment) you want to lease or buy it on hire purchase terms.

■ **Trade credit from suppliers**
Most companies use credit from suppliers to help finance their short-term business. This credit can be negotiated (the usual terms range between 30 and 90 days) and should be weighed up against the cost of losing any cash discount. Remember to weigh the cost of the discount against the cost of borrowing the sum on your overdraft. Large companies tend to use this method as a means of securing non-negotiated credit from smaller companies who have to pay interest on their loans and who can go bust while they are waiting to get paid.

■ **Medium and long-term money**

Where the aim of the business is to own the money
Many people, when they first start their own businesses, dislike the idea of raising money from strangers. They feel that it is bound to involve letting outsiders have a say in running the business. Although you must be careful about who you take money from, this fear can be exaggerated, and you can arrange your issue of shares so that they do not give any individual or group of individuals complete control over your business.

Do not put yourself in a position of having an idea and being so committed to it that you take money from anyone who will give it to you.

This is an area in which you will definitely need to take professional advice.

There are different types of shares – the main ones are:

- ordinary shares
- deferred ordinary shares
- preferred ordinary shares
- preference shares.

Ordinary shares

Here each share carries one vote and gives its owner the same proportion of the assets and profits as every other share. These ordinary shares are risk capital and the owners of ordinary shares will lose their money if the business fails and get the full rewards if it succeeds. If the company is wound up, ordinary shareholders will get nothing until all the debts have been paid including the preference shareholders. A company can issue different voting rights. It is possible to keep more than 50 per cent of the votes (and keep control of the company) and not own 50 per cent of the shares.

Ordinary shares are looked upon as permanent capital – they do not have to be repaid. However, a special 'redeemable' ordinary share can be issued – this means it can be repaid at a later date and the owner of the business has the chance of regaining full control of his business at a later date.

Deferred ordinary shares

Although these are similar to ordinary shares the owners are not entitled to the dividend until the company's profits reach a certain level which then allows them to be paid. They may possibly not be allowed to vote.

Preferred ordinary shares

These give a minimum dividend even before a company pays a dividend on its ordinary shares. They will also probably have full voting rights.

Preference shares

Preference shares are not equity although they are part of the company's own money. They pay a fixed return out of the taxed profits. This money must be paid before any dividend on the ordinary shares.

Preference shares can be 'redeemable' – this means they can be repaid at a future fixed date. They can also be convertible – i.e. converted into ordinary shares later on. Another type of preference share is the participating preference share – these shares can participate in the growth of the company once the profits have grown above a certain level. Until this point is reached they are entitled to a minimum fixed dividend. Unless the preference dividend has not been paid, preference shareholders are not normally entitled to a vote in the company's affairs or to attend company meetings.

Mortgages
Raising money on property is a traditional way of providing business finance, and a mortgage loan from a bank or building society can give you medium to long-term money at quite a reasonable cost.

Sale and leaseback of premises
Another possibility is leaseback. Here you sell the property but then rent it from the company that purchases it.

Hire purchase and instalment credit
By obtaining equipment on hire purchase you retain some ready cash that would otherwise have been tied up. Assuming that you make regular payments, your business will eventually own the equipment.

Lease
When you take out a lease you rent the equipment from another company. Although you make regular payments on the equipment it will never belong to you.

Your decision to purchase or lease will affect your tax bill so it is important to speak to your accountant about this. You will also have to think about whether it would be more suitable for your business to make one outright payment or a series of small payments over a period of time. As a new business, you may not have the money or financial security to purchase things outright.

Credit insurance and guarantee arrangements to help small exporters
There are special problems for businesses selling to overseas buyers, apart from the risks of fluctuating exchange rates. Overseas customers may be used to different credit terms and

expect to be given longer in which to pay. It is often harder to check up on their reputations and harder to get paid. You can insure against these risks with a government agency called the Export Credits Guarantee Department (see Useful addresses) or a private credit insurance company.

Project finance or joint venture finance
In this type of finance arrangement, investors provide money for a project and then get a return on their investment consisting of a percentage payment on sales. Your accountant should be able to help you find such investors.

Medium and long-term bank loans
These are used to meet permanent working capital needs and can be taken out to cover periods of up to 20 years. They must either be secured against a fixed asset or personally guaranteed by you (or another director).

Loan stocks and debentures
Loan stocks are better for larger companies. Unlike a normal loan or overdraft, where you pay the money back to the bank, this type of debt can be sold to other investors who can in turn sell it to other people. When the interest is due it will be paid to the person who finally owns the debt. Ask your accountant for advice on how to get this type of loan.

A debenture is similar to a loan stock, except that it is secured either on a fixed asset or as a floating charge. Should anything go wrong with the company, the owner of the debenture will be paid before any other of the creditors.

Convertible loan stocks
These are similar to loan stocks, except that the investor will have an option to change all or part of the loan into shares within the company.

How to approach lenders

Lenders are concerned about two things – getting regular interest payments and getting their money back. They will want security for the loan and if your business gets into trouble they will be repaid from the money you manage to get by selling these assets. They will also need to be convinced that you have the ability to make your ideas work.

Before approaching anyone for money, you must be clear about your plans. You are far more likely to succeed if you can back up your idea with facts and figures. Look at the business plan in Chapter 8 and you will see how to present your case. Different banks have different requirements and you may find that they want the information presented differently, so it is a good idea to ask about this first. Your accountant should also be able to help you with your business plan.

■ Put yourself in their shoes

Always try and put yourself in their shoes. Try and understand their point of view. The approach you take should vary according to whether you are trying to raise short or long-term finance. Don't be put off if they don't share your enthusiasm. You may have to go to a number of people before you get the money you need.

EXAMPLE

All his life Oliver had wanted to run a restaurant-cum-wine bar. He found what he thought was an ideal site, in one of the fastest-growing towns in the area. He went to see sixteen banks without success. Fortunately his patience, charm and good humour eventually paid off and he managed to get his money from one of the brewing houses.

Your backers will want to know what's in it for them. They are trying to make a profit too. Be realistic about what you intend to achieve and not over-optimistic.

■ A few golden rules

- Don't ask for less money than you really need, because it is not a good idea to go back later and ask for more. It will damage your investor's confidence in you and it will be harder to get money in the future.

- Don't just plan for the coming year. Try to think about where you want your business to be in a few years' time.

- Make sure you find the right partner(s) the first time around, especially if you are giving away shares in your business in return for the money. Your partner(s) must be able to back you in the future as well; otherwise you will be in a worse position than before.

- Never wait until you are absolutely desperate before you approach a lender. It can take a long time to get the money you need, so don't get too committed to your idea until you have the finance lined up. It can be a heartbreaking experience to put your guts into a business and then have it wrenched apart because of your own lack of judgement.

- If you're going to borrow money think about whether you want a fixed or variable rate of interest. If the interest rates drop, you don't want to find yourself locked into paying a high rate. On the other hand, you could take out a loan at a low rate and suddenly find the interest rates increasing to a point where you can no longer finance the debt.

- Coming out of a recession is not easy. Companies jostle for business and buyers play suppliers off against each other, trying to get the best terms. As your business grows, you may find it difficult to finance new orders. Make sure you arrange the money *before* this actually happens.

EXAMPLE

Susan had started her business without really thinking about the money side of it. She just plunged in and staggered on from day to day. When she was well into her project she suddenly realized that she needed more money. A friend (or an enemy?) recommended someone who was supposed to be very experienced in this particular field. She contacted him and he agreed to be a director and take on some of the financial responsibility. He put up some money in exchange for 51% ownership of the business, and he also agreed to take on some of the work. He estimated the amount of money needed in the short-term but there was no discussion about his future investment in the business.

Then, just as the first major purchases were being made, he changed his role from that of a director to an unnamed shareholder. At this stage Susan should have stopped dealing with him, because this left her with sole responsibility for the debt and without the reputation she had thought the business would acquire by having him as a director. He also hired someone else to do his share of the work, which increased the running costs of the business. In addition, this 'experienced' man got the costs, pricing and sales estimates wrong. Susan should, of course, have kept more control over things, but she didn't. The project took two years of her life, all her savings and then three years more to shake off the 'vampire'.

- **Dealing with banks**
New businesses often have different money problems from the more established ones. They may not have any security and their owners may well have no background of self-employment. For these reasons it generally takes some time for them to get started and get their cash flow right, let alone make some profit. Most banks now have departments specializing in helping small businesses, so make sure you take advantage of any advice they can give you.

Although banks may tell you that money is easy to get, this isn't always the case – it can be quite difficult and costly, especially when you're starting a new business. However it's worth shopping around – bank managers are people, and although one may turn you down another may not. Don't be put off. If you have problems getting finance, contact the Banking Information Service (see Useful addresses).

10 Vital finance questions

To organize your business finances successfully, you must be able to answer the following questions:

1. How much money have you got?

2. How much of your own money can you afford to invest in the business?

3. How much money do you need to finance your fixed assets?

4. Should you consider outright buying, leasing or hire purchase of the fixed assets?

5. How much working capital do you need to finance your current assets?

6. How much will you borrow? If you are borrowing – how do you intend to pay the money back?

7. Do you need to raise equity capital from somebody else?

8. How long will it take before you make a sale?

9. How long will it take before you're paid?

10. Will you need extra short-term money to finance temporary fluctuations, such as extra Christmas trade?

8 The business plan

The business plan sets out your ideas for your business. It should help you structure your thoughts, raise finance, and monitor the progress of your business. Its length and complexity will depend on the type of business you're starting, the level of finance you're trying to raise and who you're trying to impress.

If you're using it to raise money, the whole purpose of the report is to convince other people that you have researched the market and done your planning, that you will be able to control the finances, and that you and anyone else involved in the project are capable of getting the business on its feet and keeping it there.

Some business plans are fairly simple, while others require extensive help from an accountant. The development unit at your local Enterprise Agency should also be able to give you some assistance. There are a number of different ways a business plan can be written. The extent of the information that people require may differ and the format in which you present the material. This can be largely a matter of style. The most important thing is to present the material in a logical order and ensure that all the facts are there. Keep any technical language to a minimum and support your main document, if necessary, with additional information, such as technical processes, market research reports and so on.

Reports are written in a style that can sometimes be difficult to catch on to. You should use the third person rather than the first

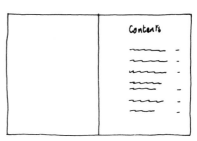

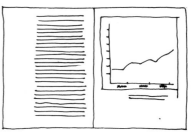

person. For example, instead of saying, 'I have decided' say, 'It has been decided that . . .' Above all, your business plan must be intelligible and readable. If a potential investor can't understand what you're saying, you will find it difficult to get any funding.

Before you start to write your buiness plan, draw up a page plan. Once you have created a structure, you'll find it easier to handle the information and keep each section to a reasonable length. Number the pages and write the title of each topic at the top of the page.

The cover

The cover should look professional and the material should be properly bound. It should be typed on to A4 white paper.

On the cover, type the following:

BUSINESS PLAN

Presented to:

Presented by:

Date:

You will need to do a separate cover for each investor to whom you present your plan.

Summary

At the front of your business plan you should provide a summary of all the most important facts. Ideally it should be no longer than a page (or two at the most) and it should contain the following information: the purpose of the business plan; a brief description of the products or services being offered; the market (why you think there will be a demand and what you anticipate sales to be); a summary of the financial projections; the funding you require; any equity you'll be giving for outside investment; how the money will be spent; your professional background and contact phone number and address.

Contents

Follow this with a detailed list of contents (including page numbers) to help people find their way around the report more easily.

Here is an example, showing how you might present your list of contents:

What to include in your business plan

Here are some general hints about what sort of information you should include under the various headings in your business plan.

1. Introduction

1.1 Background to the proposal
This is a clear statement giving the reader an outline of the business. This differs from the summary in that it provides extensive and detailed information that the reader can turn to should they decide to read on.

1.2 History of the business
If the business has been running for some time you'll need to add a separate section giving its history. This should include a brief description of its products or services, profit and loss to date, and a valuation of its current assets.

2. The product or service

Describe your product or service. Say why it is new or different, and discuss its strengths and weaknesses. Say how it can be used and describe its properties and features (without getting too technical). Say whether there is any research and development that needs to be completed. Say which legal requirements you must comply with, and whether there are any statutory or advisory standards that have to be met. State whether any patents or intellectual property rights are necessary to protect your idea, and whether you have applied for them. Include any long-term plans for further development of your product or service.

3. The market

3.1 Market research
Write down the results of the general research you have carried out. Give the current market size and the demand for similar products/services, and show the anticipated market trend. Give a short summary of the results of any consumer research you have carried out. (The main bulk of your research will go into the Appendices.)

3.2 Competition

Explain who your competitors are, and point out their strengths and weaknesses. Discuss these points under the following headings:

- Product/service
- Customer segmentation
- Pricing
- Packaging
- Distribution
- Selling
- Sales promotion
- Advertising
- PR
- Future developments

You may also want to discuss their financing, research and development, premises, plant and equipment, and personnel. Make sure you give a critical comparison. Include drawings or photographs if you have them.

■ 4. Marketing plan

4.1 Customer segmentation

Describe your customers (e.g. their social grade/class, age, occupation, etc.). Say why your product/service will satisfy their particular needs. State how many there are and how many you can reach.

4.2 Pricing

Give the price of your product/service, and the reasons for choosing that price. Discuss your costs, margins and discounts.

4.3 Packaging

If you intend to use packaging, describe it. Say what sort of packaging you intend to provide, the labelling requirements and costs.

4.4 Distribution
Discuss the geographical area you need to cover, storage facilities, method of delivery and transportation. Give the costs.

4.5 Selling
Discuss your method of selling, your plans and costs.

4.6 Sales promotion
If you use sales promotion, your scheme must add value to your product or service. Write down your ideas under these headings:

- Objective – what you intend to achieve.
- Strategy – how you will do it.
- Costs – how much it will cost.
- Time – when you intend to do it.
- Results – how you will assess the results.

4.7 Advertising
Write down your ideas under the same headings you used for sales promotion in 4.6.

4.8 Public relations
Write down your ideas under the same headings you used for sales promotion in 4.6.

■ 5. Financial information

5.1 Capital expenditure
This should include the amount that needs to be spent, and when it needs to be spent, on major items such as premises, plant and vehicles.

5.2 Financial forecasts
You need to write this section in detail, whether you plan to use the business plan to monitor your performance or to raise money. Either way, this section could make or break you. Try doing it yourself and then go through it with a professional accountant. The more familiar you are with the financial data the better off

you'll be, both in discussions to obtain finance and also in the day-to-day control of your business. Options differ on how many years ahead you should forecast (usually from one to five years). This will depend on the type of business you're starting and the amount of money involved. Take professional advice.

In this section you need to include your profit and loss, cash flow forecast and balance sheet. (See Chapter 6 for details of how to prepare these documents.)

You should also include a note on your break-even date and the key assumptions you have made in preparing your forecasts. Include a comment on how sensitive you think the forecasts will be to any internal changes (such as failing to meet production targets) or external changes (such as a problem with a supplier or failing to meet sales targets).

5.3 *Funding*
In this section you need to include: any current shareholding structure; the amount of funding you require and when; the purpose to which the money will be put; the potential sources (internally from you or other founders, or externally from bank loans, grants, loan capital, etc); the proposed shareholding structure after funding; any security available for external investors; any proposed managerial participation in the business by external investors (such as reporting, cheque signing, etc). It is suggested that you take professional advice here, as this is a complicated subject.

■ 6. Personnel
If you are working with other people, you must say what each person will be doing. This means providing a management and staffing structure. You will have to say what skills you will need in the beginning and in the second and third years. You should also give brief details of present key personnel and their previous experience. Include full *curricula vitae* in the Appendices. Give the costs and any special terms of employment. Include details of your professional advisers in the Appendices.

■ **7. Premises**
Say where you will be working from and the premises you may need in the future. Give the size, special requirements, location and probable costs.

■ **8. Manufacturing process**
If your business is at all technical, explain the process in simple terms. Describe where your materials will come from and include comments on the reliability of your suppliers and subcontractors. Make sure you mention any potential problems with the manufacturing process, including noise and environmental contaminants.

You should also give some idea of what after-sales service and maintenance agreements you will be offering.

■ **9. Risks**
It is always better to identify the risks yourself. There is nothing worse than having a potential investor sit there and point out your weaknesses to you. All confidence in you will immediately evaporate.

■ **10. Appendices**
Include the technical details, marketing reports, *curricula vitae* and anything that is too bulky to go into the main body of the report.

■ **11. Time scale**
It is essential to put in a time scale for your business plan. Plot each action against the month you intend to do it.

9 How to create a corporate image

You will by now have a pretty good idea of who your customers are. You should know how you're going to differentiate yourself from your competitors, you should know your price, and have a clear idea of what benefits your product or service will be offering. All this information is vital when it comes to creating your corporate image.

A corporate image doesn't simply refer to the design of a company's letterhead. In reality a corporate image goes much deeper and covers the way a business relates to its whole social and cultural context. This is especially important if you are thinking of marketing in another country or going into a line of work you are not totally familiar with.

If you think of the word 'corporate' as meaning all aspects of the business united into one body, you'll get some idea of the importance of this idea. A corporate image envelopes the whole organization. Its essence should be conveyed to people working inside the organization and anyone in contact with it from outside, such as suppliers, customers or members of the public.

■■■■■■■■■ Personal image

When you start your own business people will perceive *you* as being the business. The way you conduct yourself verbally, non-verbally and visually will give people a clear statement of who you are and what sort of business you are running.

The clothes you wear, the way you speak, your tone of voice, the words you use, your body language, all give the world a message about you. Some people don't have a very clear picture of themselves, and it can come as quite a shock to realize that they are being, consciously or unconsciously, assessed in this way. If you haven't considered your image recently perhaps it is time you asked someone to tell you what sort of impression you give.

When you receive this reaction try and think about it in relation to the type of impression you want to give your customers about your business. Consider whether there will be any conflict between your own personal image and the image you're trying to create for your business.

This process is in no way superficial, it will involve you in reflecting on the behavioural aspects of the way you intend to conduct your business, how you will take on your role, how this conflicts with your ordinary personality, and the hopes and wishes your customers will have when you are playing your role and carrying out a task for them.

Each role carries a persona. This persona is a collective phenomenon and is a facet of the personality. Because it is collective it could equally belong to anyone else. For example, we expect a certain type of persona from a person playing the role of a nurse, another type from a person in the role of a waiter, a builder, a gardener, a counsellor, a painter and so on. To some extent people fit the role they feel most happy in, but the persona is never the whole person. It is, however, a necessity, through which we relate to the world. It indicates what we may expect from other people but there is a danger of identifying with it too much. To maintain a healthy, balanced approach, you need to be able to take on the necessary persona at work without letting it overwhelm your ordinary personality. That way you can retain your natural flexibility and adapt to change when it occurs.

Business image

The name of your company, the price of your product/service, your advertising material and the place you sell from, all say something about your business and what it stands for. Together they form a persona for your business that people can identify with, or project their own fantasies on to. Think about creating a mask. The mask is a social self, which stands for the difference between one's own thoughts and other people's understanding of one's personality. A corporate image, apart from helping your customers get a clear idea about you, will give you some very clear benefits as well, such as protecting your inner and possibly, more vulnerable you.

Every time we make a purchase we make a statement about ourselves. What we choose to wear, the furniture we buy, the pictures we hang on our walls, the food in our cupboards, the shops we go to, all give people an idea of who we are. (For example, think of someone carrying a Harrods bag and write down what goes through your mind.) We buy things because, consciously or unconsciously, we think they suit the image we want to project or introject.

■ Creating a corporate image
Before you create your corporate image, think about the personality you want your business to have. If you don't think about it very carefully you may end up telling people completely the wrong thing. This is an area in which most people who are starting a business make three mistakes: they fail to see their corporate image from the consumer's point of view; they don't spend enough money on their corporate image; or they try to design it themselves.

Creating your own business requires so much emotional energy that you become almost blind to what is being created. You become the work and the work becomes you – there is little or no objectivity. When you start to create your corporate image it is vital to see it from other people's point of view. Otherwise you can end up with a business name, slogan and image that is full of meaning for you but comes across as complete nonsense to anyone else.

In addition, many people who start their own businesses are doing it on a shoestring and they don't see the importance of spending the little they do have on decent letterhead and notepaper. If you find yourself skimping, remember that customers will be using your notepaper as a way of getting an impression of your business and the quality of your product or service.

Many people think they can save money by designing their letterhead themselves. They don't understand that it takes a designer years of training to be able to do this job. Depending on who you get and what you want, getting a professional designer does not have to cost a lot of money. It is probably the single most important thing you could do to start your business in a professional way. So start shopping around now.

■ **Choosing a corporate image**
You can base your corporate image on your personal image and/or the name of your business.

Choose a name that is easy to say, easy to design, easy to remember, and says something about your business. Remember to check that it hasn't been used by any of your competitors. Check the relevant directories and contact Companies House (see Useful addresses) and make sure no one else has it registered as a Trade Mark. You also need to ensure that you are complying with all the provisions of the Business Names Act 1985 (see the section on 'Business Names' in Chapter 5).

You may also want a company slogan and a symbol or logo. Other points to consider when getting your letterhead designed include lettering or typeface, paper quality and colour. These should all be chosen to reflect your business persona.

■ **Briefing the designer**
If you want a good job done, give the designer proper instructions. If you give bad instructions, you'll get bad work back. Try and get the designer to do more than one rough design for you to choose from. You can find the names of designers in the *Yellow Pages*. Look at their previous work and see if you like their style.

When you go to a designer make sure that you give him or her all the information needed to create a design that will accurately reflect your business.

- State your objectives. The designer must know what the design is going to be used for. For instance, if you want the design to be used on packaging and promotional material as well as letterhead, compliment slip and calling card, the designer needs to make sure that it can be enlarged or reduced and keep its impact.

- Say what your business specializes in. Give a clear statement of the primary product/service offered by your organization.

- Describe the main benefits (selling points) of the product/service.

- Say how your product/service differs from the competition.

- Give a description of your customers (social grade/class, age, occupation, etc).

- Describe the place/places you will be selling from.

- Give your price and say where it stands in relation to the competition.

- Provide samples of your competitors' selling material. This will enable the designer to design something that will position you competitively in the market. When potential customers get a letter from you they will be able to compare the feelings and thoughts they get from your letter with those they have received from your competitors.

- Choose the adjectives that most accurately describe your business persona. Do you want to be seen as: modern, dynamic, approachable, traditional, local, international, scientific, responsible, interesting, enterprising, national, efficient, creative, caring, hygienic, cheap, exclusive, professional, fashionable, original, safe, healthy, quick, friendly, convenient, trendy, educational, formal, relaxed, or anything else? List the adjectives in order of importance.

- Choose a business name. Remember to choose one that is easy to say, easy to design, easy to remember and says something about your business. Check that it's legal and hasn't already been used by one of your competitors. Use your personal name unless it really is very odd. Sometimes it's better to use a trading name to add a professional gloss. For instance, if you want to appear bigger than you are, you could add 'and Associates' or 'Consultancy'. If you live at a house called 'Lovers' Nest' or something similar and you're working from home, you can change your address by writing to your local Royal Mail Customer Care Office.

- Decide whether you want a symbol. Some people think they need to have a symbol or logo. This often incorporates their initials (not generally a good idea, as it means something to you and nothing to anybody else) or some abstract idea that they feel will give people a sense of what their business is all about. Unless you have enough money to imbue these initials, signs and images with meaning, don't use them. Try and keep things simple and choose something that is in common usage and means something to everyone. For instance, if you're starting a nursery school, and you want to communicate a caring, loving, safe, patient, motherly business persona, you would choose a symbol to reflect all this, such as a tree or a crescent moon. The name could then be developed from this – The Tree Nursery School or The Crescent Nursery School. Don't panic if you can't incorporate a symbol into your design. The name and typeface you use, the colour of the ink and the quality of the paper can perform a similar task. Speak to your designer.

- Decide whether you want a slogan. A slogan is quite useful for certain types of business but it is not always necessary. Like your business name, it should be memorable and reflect your business persona. Once you've thought of a slogan, try it out on a few potential customers and see how they react. When you've made a decision, ask the designer to incorporate the slogan into the overall design.

- If you're VAT registered, remember to give the designer your VAT number. This must appear on all your stationery.

Above all, you must be happy with your business name and your corporate image. But your customers must be as well. This is sometimes a difficult balance to strike. Although amusing names and slogans can occasionally be effective, humour needs to be treated very carefully, as shown by the following story.

EXAMPLE

Joe was starting a business selling shoes to elderly people in retirement homes. He had a great sense of humour and one of the names that he thought about but later discarded was 'Feet First' . . .

10 How to promote your business

When you create any promotional material you must keep a 'family likeness' (remember your corporate image). Your promotional material must also be truthful and legal. The Advertising Standards Authority keeps an eye out for people who breach the law, and they can be quite tough. If you're in doubt, check with your Enterprise Agency.

Types of promotion

Each way of promoting a business has its own characteristics and costs and you will need to bear these in mind when deciding which ones to use. Here's a list of the main types of promotion:

- Advertising
  This covers advertising in the media (in national newspapers, local newspapers, magazines, trade journals, directories, radio, TV and cinema) and outside advertising (on bill boards, buses/tubes/taxis, display boards and shop windows).

- Signage
  Promotional signage includes office signs, shop fascias, window signs, display signs, labels and vehicle livery.

- Sales literature
  This includes leaflets, brochures and other sales aids,

such as price lists, videos, tapes, fact sheets, price lists, and testimonial letters from satisfied customers.

- Public relations
  Gifts, cards, trade shows, exhibitions, press releases, news summaries, photographs with captions, sponsorship and public speaking are all forms of public relations promotion.

- Sales promotion
  Sales promotion includes special offers, competitions and samples.

- Direct marketing
  The main types are direct mail, telemarketing and direct-response advertising.

- Personal selling
  This covers any form of face-to-face selling.

- Stationery
  Business cards, letterheads, reports, binding, continuation sheets, invoices, statements, quotations, estimates and envelopes all show your company name and are therefore forms of promotion.

- Presentation
  This includes your corporate image, wrappers and containers, display material, the way your premises look, the personal behaviour of you and your staff, the style and tone of your letters and the way in which you handle telephone calls. Letters are very important and you will need to pay special attention to the way they are written and presented.

How to decide which forms of promotion to pay for

Some methods of promotion are ongoing. Others are used for specific purposes and their benefits need to be weighed up against their costs.

You should begin by thinking about your market segments (as

identified in Chapter 2) and which methods could best be used to contact these particular groups of customers. Please bear in mind that you may be starting a business where you will only be dealing with one segment, or that you can approach all your segments using the same method of promotion. You may, on the other hand, be the type of business which will benefit from carrying out this exercise very carefully because each segment will need to be approached differently.

Segment 1   Segment 2   Segment 3

1. Name the segment/s

2. Percentage of business

3. Product/service features

4. Benefits

5. Price

6. Promotion:
   Advertising?
   Sales literature?
   Sales promotion?
   Public relations?
   What about the competition?

7. Place

Not all businesses use the same methods to promote themselves. It is always a good idea to study what your competitors are doing, as this will give you an idea of the methods used in your type of business.

For example, the entertainment industry mainly uses posters, direct mail, leaflets and press advertisements. Business courses are usually promoted by direct mail and personal selling. Shops use posters in their windows and press advertisements. Manufacturers of consumer goods put more money into advertising, then sales promotion, then selling, followed by public relations. Industrial companies put most of their money into personal selling, then sales promotion, advertising and public relations. Some businesses may be more price-sensitive than others. Take advice from your Enterprise Agency, a marketing consultant or an advertising agency before you make your choice.

How much should you spend?

If you decide how many people you want to influence, and what you want them to do as a result of seeing your advertisement, then you're off to a good start. In practice, the amount you spend will depend on how much money you have, and what you need to spend to achieve your goals. (The first method sadly ignores the effect promotion can have on sales volume, but it is the reality that most people starting their own businesses have to contend with.)

Find out what your competitors are spending if you can, but remember that this doesn't necessarily mean they've got it right. When you have some comparative sales figures you will be able to get an idea of the effect advertising has, but don't use this as a formula for the rest of your business life. Some methods of promotion are easier to check on than others. For example, if you phone 100 people and get ten sales, you know that in the future you are likely to have to make 100 calls to get ten sales. It's the same with direct mail; you can immediately judge its success by the response you get. It is difficult to do this with media advertising. As someone once said, they knew advertising worked, but which half worked they had yet to find out!

Unless you have a lot of money to invest and you are pretty sure of the response rate, and you can match what your competitors are spending, it's best to avoid business ideas that require a great deal of expensive media advertising.

Having said this, if you are pretty sure of the likely response rate, and you're prepared to take the risk, it may be a good way to get yourself established. Life would be great if for every £100 you spent on promotion you got £1000 worth of business. It is by no means pleasant to spend £100 and only get £50 worth of business back. However this may be something you have to accept while you are establishing yourself; it will take time for people to get to know about your business and you may need to experiment.

Sadly there are no hard and fast rules. You may find it helpful to think of advertising not as a cost but as an investment which will enable you to announce the birth of your business and nurture it as it grows. As the business matures the amount you invest will change and your promotional methods should as well. Always record the results of any promotional effort and analyse them carefully. This information will be essential in planning your future promotional spending.

How do you make your promotion effective?

The essence of promotion is communication, and effective communication means getting your message across to the right people. These are the steps you need to follow:

- Look at the way you have segmented your market. Deciding on your target audience will influence what is said, who says it, how it is said and where it is said.

- Think about the response you want.
  Obviously you want your target audience to buy from you, but buying decisions are made up of a long process of decision making. This means they must be aware of you in the first place, then show some interest in what you have to offer. You need to think about where your customers stand in terms of their decision to buy. When you start your own business, although some of your customers will not know anything about you, others may know you from before and it is obvious that those people need to be treated differently.

- Choose the right message.

Frame your message in a way your target audience will understand, taking into account their likely interpretation of it.

- Choose the media most likely to reach them.

- Find a way of checking the response to your message.

How to use the different methods of promotion

■ Advertising

When you advertise you are making your customers aware of your
business and helping them to compare you with your competitors.
With advertising you can repeat your message over and over again
and extensive advertising says something about your popularity
and success. It creates product awareness and knowledge, builds
sales and reassures buyers. It reaches a great number of people in
a large geographical area and can be used in a number of ways: it
can help you dramatize your business and bring it alive; it can
build up your image; and it can be used to trigger quick sales (as in
retail advertising). But it is impersonal, it can be very costly,
people may ignore it and it lacks the persuasiveness of personal
selling.

How to create an advertisement
As a general rule, if you have to choose between size and the
number of times you can afford to place your ad, go for half the
size and twice the number of insertions. Most small businesses
can't afford to advertise all the time so as a general rule
concentrate your efforts in short bursts throughout the year.

Certain positions in papers and magazines get more attention than
others. Talk to the advertising salesperson about this.

When you create your advertisements you should keep a family
likeness – the same typeface, border, slogan, writing style and
layout. If you want to say something new, change only the
headline or the copy – nothing else. Headlines should grab
people's attention and make them say 'Tell me more!'. If you're
creating an advertisement and you don't have money to spend on
creating different campaigns, keep the same design and the same
image as this help people to recognize you.

Ads with pictures get more attention. Demonstrate the product or
show the reward people get when they use it. Keep them smiling!
Show what the product makes, or the effect it has. For example, if
you're selling a drill, show the hole the drill makes. It you're
selling dandruff shampoo, show a happy person with healthy hair,

being kissed. It's important to convey the positive atmosphere or the benefits people get from using the product or service.

Your language must be clear. Don't use long words and if you're selling something scientific don't explain how it works in the headline. People need to be able to scan and absorb the information in headlines very quickly.

Use the present tense. Tell the truth and don't exaggerate. Keep the typeface simple and easy to read. Write the way you would speak if you had the customer right in front of you. Imagine that you can see them sitting there. Always use plain English and avoid fancy or unfamiliar words. The average reading age of people living in Great Britain is around 11 years old, so it's best to use short words, short sentences and short paragraphs.

However, you must still treat people as intelligent human beings. Make sure the advertisement tells them what to do without sounding patronizing, and always use the word 'you' wherever possible.

Here's a structure to follow when writing an advertisement:

- Give the name of the product/service and describe it.

- Say how people will benefit from using it.

- Tell them why your product/service is different.

- Repeat the benefits.

- Repeat the name.

If you're using the creative services of a newspaper or an instant print service, do make sure that your advertisement does not look like everyone else's. Give them clear instructions, and pay a little extra if necessary, to ensure that your advertisement stands out from the rest.

■ **Sales promotion**
Sales promotion is used to create a quick response. Although it tends to attract attention and increase sales in the short term it is not as effective as advertising in building up a long-term preference. It covers special offers and discounts, money-off

vouchers, coupons, contests and so on. It can provide excitement and interest by giving extra value and it should be combined with some form of advertising to tell people about the special offer.

- **Public relations**

Stories about your business that appear in the press, or on radio or television, carry an authority that advertisements don't have. People tend to believe what they see and hear in the media. The message tends to reach people who avoid salespeople and advertising as it gets presented in the media as news. Properly used, this sort of publicity can gain your business at least as much attention as advertising. But you do have to keep making fresh news, as the media are only interested in what is new.

Unlike placing an advertisement, you do not have to pay for the space and a properly planned public relations campaign can be very effective. However, it is also the method of promotion that you will have least control over. Stories that you write are likely to be changed by editors and they sometimes don't turn out exactly the way you anticipated. You will also have to learn how to handle any negative publicity, should it come your way.

Dealing with the media

Preparing a list
Prepare a list of the newspapers, magazines, trade journals, radio and TV programmes that you think would be interested in telling their audience about you or your business activities.

Then get the names of the editors or journalists interested in your subject and give them a ring. Or you could take a chance and send the material off, then follow up with a phone call. Tailor your release to each media outlet – don't send the same one to all of them.

The four main ways of presenting your information are as a news release, a short statement, a photograph with a caption, or a summary.

Writing a news release

Use news releases when you are starting out, or have something new to say about your business. If you use more than one page, number and headline the second page and write 'continued' at the bottom of the first page. Use double spacing and wide margins.

Make sure the information is presented in a logical order and that each paragraph is not too long (about 50 words). Try to use quotations so that it sounds realistic, as if the journalist has spoken to someone who is truly involved in the business. Be positive about your business; at the same time try and make it sound objective. Write on your own letterhead and make sure everything is spelt correctly.

Begin with the words 'News Release from . . .' (give your business name, address and phone number). Give the date and a release date. Do not request any delay in publication – it may deter the editor from using your story. Then follow this structure:

- Headline
  Make up a simple headline – don't worry if it isn't witty.

- First paragraph
  Briefly summarize your whole story in the first paragraph. Make it interesting so that it grabs the reader's attention.

- Second paragraph
  Describe why your product/service is different, and state the advantages. Make it personal so people can see the benefits.

- Third paragraph
  Say who will want to use the product/service, and why.

- Fourth paragraph
  Give a description of the product/service and state the price. Don't use jargon!

- Fifth paragraph
  Say where the product/service can be bought.

- Identification
  At the bottom of the page write 'End' and say who the news release has been written by (give name, job title and phone number).

Writing a short statement
Send in a short statement when you want to announce the following: an exhibition, a gift to charity, participation in a local event, change of address, staff achievement, staff promotion or appointment of new staff. A short statement is generally between one sentence and one paragraph long.

Presenting a photograph and caption
A good photograph can be used on its own, or with another type of story. Label the photograph on the back with your name, address and phone number. A caption pasted on the back should describe the event. Don't use paper clips or staples because these will damage the picture. Send glossy photos, not matt or glazed, about 8 in. × 6 in. or 10 in. × 8 in. The press will sometimes send their own photographer; do ask them along to events as their photographs are more likely to be used.

Writing a summary
Some businesses need to present detailed technical information. Write a short summary of such details and enclose the full report so that the editor can refer back to it if necessary.

After publication
Once a press release of yours has been published make sure you keep the article in your sales folder. This together with any letters from satisfied customers, will be a powerful tool in any sales presentation.

Personal appearances and corporate hospitality
This covers speaking at meetings, joining business clubs, sending gifts and cards to clients, taking customers out for lunch and generally putting yourself in places where people can get to know you and where you are able to talk about yourself and find out about other people. Think about the relationships efforts you

should make with people or organizations you will have contact with in the course of your business – such as your local Council, Training and Enterprise Council, Enterprise Agency, local college, bank manager, neighbours and so on.

Trade shows and exhibitions

Trade shows are an ideal way to meet new customers. If you can get to the right trade show you will have the opportunity to introduce yourself to a concentrated group of people who are interested in finding out about new businesses. The people looking after your stand must be properly briefed and your leaflets should be in a place where people can pick them up easily. As the main purpose of being at a show is to make new contacts, you must try and get the names and addresses of every person who visits your stand. Make sure you prepare a news release and have photographs of your stand. Send your publicity material to the relevant media (and sales representatives if you have them), and to your existing and potential customers. You could try offering refreshments and asking people over to join you. Buy a portable display stand that you can use again. This will help people recognize and remember you.

Apart from going to large trade shows, you can set up your own exhibitions by displaying your products in a hotel, public hall, library, shop, or the foyer of a busy building. You could also hire a hall and send out invitations to potential customers. If you have finished a particular job of work (such as a garden shed or a conservatory), ask your customer if you can invite people round to see it and/or take photographs for publication. (You may have to offer them some inducement, such as a discount on the price.)

Sponsorship

If you want to build a relationship with your local community you could support activities in your area, such as music festivals, sport, prizes, conferences, to name but a few. Make sure the people attending the event are customers or potential customers.

■ **Direct marketing**
In direct marketing you interact directly with your potential

customers. If you're considering using this method you must make sure that your product is selling at a price that will cover your costs. The response to this sort of marketing is generally very low – on average 2% – but it can go down to nothing or almost nothing. It is essential to work out a realistic response rate.

Direct mail and mail-order catalogue
With this method you buy a mailing list and send a single advertisement, sample, letter or catalogue to your potential customers. Some businesses even send video tapes.

Working out the costs
As a general rule, and this will differ from business to business, you will spend a third on advertising, a third on producing the item and a third on overheads and profit. You will need to pay for: premises; the mailing (catalogues, leaflets and letter writing, design, artwork, proofs, paper and printing, renting and/or buying lists, order forms, envelopes, putting the mailing together and postage); the goods (cost of the goods, packaging, postage, storage and insurance). You also need to allow for people sending goods back if they don't like them and claiming they haven't received the goods.

Getting the addresses
You can build your own list of addresses from directories, advertisements, etc., or you can buy or rent a list. Once you have been in business for a while, you can use your own records. If possible, you should try to build up a database of addresses on a word-processor or computer so that you can print out the labels whenever you need them. For more information on this, write to the Direct Marketing Association (see Useful addresses).

■ Direct-response marketing

Telemarketing
You can use telemarketing on its own or to supplement your existing personal selling. There are companies that specialize in

selling over the telephone. You can set your own up or use existing services. Ask your Enterprise Agency for information.

Direct-response advertising
Direct-response advertising on television describes the product and gives customers a number to phone (free of charge). You can also use this method in other media, such as newspapers, radio and magazines.

■ **Personal selling**
Unless you organize your business so that you never meet your customers face-to-face (for example by only selling through the post), personal selling will be one of your most important promotional tools. As this is the method that new businesses use most frequently, the subject is considered in more detail in Chapter 11. It is a good idea to get some special training in this area, as personal selling has some unique characteristics and most small business owners have to be able to do it. It involves you in an intimate relationship with your customers, in which you are able to observe and judge their reactions. This helps you to adjust your selling methods, and what you're selling, to meet your customers' needs and build up a good long-term relationship.

Planning

When you have decided on the best way to promote your business you'll need to draw up a promotional plan. This will form part of your business plan (described in Chapter 8). Draw a grid, with the months of the year at the top, and work out what you'll be doing, when you'll be doing it and how much it will cost. Don't do anything without thinking: Objectives – what do I want to achieve? Strategy – what is the best way to go about it? Time – when shall I do it? Cost – how much will it cost? Control – how can I assess whether what I am doing is successful?

11 How to be a successful salesperson

If you haven't sold before, you may have some grotesque ideas of what selling is all about. Understandably, people who have had bad experiences with salespeople don't often like the idea of selling because they think they will have to operate in a similar way. If your thoughts about selling are dominated by this stereotype of the self-interested, bulldozing, fast-talking, dishonest salesperson, get rid of it now because it will prevent you developing your ability to promote yourself and your business. If you don't sell, your business will die a quick death. It is essential that you learn to play this role or find somebody else to do it for you.

For a successful sale to take place: people must want what you have to offer; they must like and trust you; and they must have the money and be able to take the decision to spend it. Don't waste your time on people who do not meet these criteria; there are plenty of people who will. And never insist that anyone buys anything.

Before you start selling, find out who influences or makes the decision to buy. Don't chat up the wrong person. Remember – for a person to buy, they must like you, they must want your product or service, they must have the money and be able to take a decision to buy. Research is the key to success. Identify your best customer segment and concentrate on it. Find out where your greatest opportunities are and who you should be speaking to.

Some people find it easier to sell tangible products and others find it easier to sell intangible services. It is important to recognize your own preferences and choose the right business to start up in.

Successful salespeople are absolutely honest with themselves and their customers. They don't try to deceive people or cheat them. To be a truly effective salesperson you must be genuinely concerned about your customers' well-being. People will not buy from you unless they are convinced that you are acting in their best interests.

■ The way you feel

The key element in selling is enthusiasm. Good selling involves transferring your emotional commitment and belief in yourself to the other person. The more enthusiastic you are, the easier it will be for you to sell. You must believe in what you're selling and believe in yourself as well.

You also need to reflect on which aspects of the selling role make you feel uncomfortable, because this will get in the way of your performing it to the best of your ability. Think about what feelings and thoughts are getting in your way. For example, some people find it difficult to pick up the phone, while other people find it difficult to ask for the order. If you want to develop your ability to sell you must try doing what you're afraid of. Every time you do this and succeed, you will find it a little easier to do the next time.

Make a few calls. So what, if nobody wants to talk to you. Yes, it is frustrating but it doesn't hurt. People may say no, but it won't cause you any lasting pain. And the next time around you'll be more relaxed and find it easier. Some people say 'I can't do this' or 'I'm bad at that', and as long as you say you're bad at something you'll believe it. Stop running yourself down. If you feel bad about yourself you'll find it difficult to sell. It is important to feel good about yourself! The better you feel, the better you'll do. Before every sales call say to yourself, 'I am going to make this sale, they are going to love it, I'm really good at selling, everything is going to be great! I'm going to make this sale!'

When you feel good about yourself you will believe in your ability to sell. You will then come across as cool, calm and relaxed, absolutely confident in yourself and your ability to provide a top-class product or service. This can be difficult when you're not doing very well, but you have to overcome your negative feelings. If you go in to see a customer and you're feeling gloomy it is highly unlikely that you will make a sale. All you'll succeed in doing is making them feel as miserable as you!

All salespeople are frightened of customers saying no, and as most sales calls do end in a no, self-employment is going to be pretty insufferable if you can't cope with this sort of rejection. Lack of success increases the fear of rejection and creates a vicious circle. If you're going to succeed you need to be able to cope with people saying no. You have to remember that they are not saying no to you, they are saying no to your product or service. If you take it personally you'll withdraw from contacting customers altogether, find excuses and kill time having coffee, visiting a friend and so on – anything rather than face another brush-off. Don't give up until you're victorious. When you make your first sale you will feel great and this will help you to make your next sale.

When you have completed a sales call immediately think about what you did right and what you did wrong. You will then be able to work out what you ought to change and how you could do better in the future. Don't carry your disappointments with you because they will only pull you down. Resolve to change and leave it at that. If in the long run you find that you are not able to do this, think about getting someone else to help you.

A few golden rules of selling

■ **Prepare what you're going to say**
Don't say the first thing that comes into your head. Prepare what you're going to say and rehearse it before you pick up the phone or go in for a meeting. Say it over and over again until the words fall out of your mouth warmly and naturally. Customers can be quite antagonistic when you first approach them, so you must find a way to express yourself that will not put them on the defensive. Learn how to introduce yourself and interest people in your first few words. Find out what your customers want, understand their problems and understand their reasons for buying.

■ **First impressions count**

As soon as customers see or hear you, they immediately begin to form an impression of the sort of person you are. Your voice, clothes, general tidiness and body language will predetermine their attitude towards you. Customers expect you to behave in a certain way. They will listen to your tone of voice and your choice of words; they will watch for your smile and take in your emotions through your body language. Sometimes these non-verbal messages are much more effective than words. Most of the way we communicate is non-verbal. When you listen, look attentive, lean forward slightly and nod and smile so that they know you're listening. Make sure the surroundings are pleasant and that you're not interrupted. If you're on their premises, ask them if there is somewhere quiet that you can go.

■ **Good manners means good business**

People want to like the person they buy from. Do everything you can to make them like you. If someone leaves a message for you to call them back, phone as soon as you can, however unimportant it seems. It is good manners and it will also help build your reputation for efficiency. A nobody today could be a somebody tomorrow. Treat everyone as if he or she were your most important customer.

Make sure that you're consistently warm, courteous, patient, tactful and prompt and that everything about you gives people that message. As much for your own sense of pride as anything else, it's good to know that whenever you look in a mirror, you like what you see.

■ **Be prompt and efficient**

Customers appreciate having their time valued. Like it or not, most people are in a hurry. Good service means doing things promptly. On the other hand, spending a lot of time with a customer can also be seen as a sign of respect; it depends on your relationship with them, the situation and the type of person. You should also make sure your workplace is well organized so that you can find what you need quickly and efficiently.

- **Know your market and your product**

  You must know about your own and your competitors' products. You must know how their prices compare with yours and how your products differ. You must be aware of their strengths and weaknesses. You must know everything about what you're selling and you will not be able to sell well until you also know exactly how your product or service will satisfy your customers' needs. Don't ever knock the competition. Just say, 'I know the competition provide an excellent service but some of their customers have come to us. Would you like to know why?'

- **Find out what the customers' needs are**

  A successful salesperson does not sell, they only make it easier for their customers to buy. People buy for their reasons, not our reasons. Professional selling starts when you find out what your customers' needs are. Then you can match what your customers want with what you can supply. You have to be able to show them how they will gain from using your product or service. People buy benefits, not features.

  If you ask people carefully thought questions you'll discover what they want and they'll tell you what they like or dislike about your product or service. Ask them how they order, which products they buy, when they buy them, who they buy them from, what they like, why they like it, and so on. Give them all your attention and try to see everything from their point of view. Find out what they want and what is stopping them making a decision to buy. Once you have found out what they want, you can keep supplying them with it.

- **Anticipate objections**

  As a general rule, you will not be able to make a sale without encountering a number of objections. Objections are part of the selling game. Instead of seeing them as obstacles, you can reframe them in order to reveal a different meaning in what people are saying. For example, 'I can't afford this' may mean 'Can you tell me how I can find the money?' It could be seen as an invitation to tell them about any credit or discount you might be able to offer.

  Take every objection and use it as a request for more information.

Don't get defensive and see an objection as an attack on you. See it as the beginning of the negotiation. Listen to what the customer is saying even though you have heard the same objection 100 times before. Tell them that they have brought up an important issue and take what they say seriously. The way in which you handle their objections may well determine whether you make the sale or not. Think what objections people could possibly have and work out logical answers to each of them. Don't make up an answer on the spot while you're making your sale; think it out before.

Don't argue with customers or make them feel they're in the wrong. If you sense that you're not getting the business because of unspoken objections, try getting people to talk more. Always face your fears and bring the objections out into the open where they can be discussed. Don't argue or brush these objections aside; spend time talking them through honestly.

If you don't succeed immediately, take a longer-term approach. Send them a Christmas card and go back again later. Try not to let them say no. Keep the door open.

Making a sale

■ Getting the order

This is the most difficult and stressful part of any sales presentation. The customer may be frightened of taking the wrong decision and you are frightened of finally being rejected.

Most salespeople have to ask for the order a number of times. You need to judge when the time is right by looking out for the buying signals: changes in attitude, changes in body language, and so on. It is no use thinking that you can get away with only asking for the order once. Do what you're frightened of doing: ask for the order. There is no better way of overcoming your fears than doing what you don't like doing.

Don't think that when your potential customers say they want to think it over they are really going home to think about it. The moment they lose sight of you they will forget who you are and what you have said. When they say they want to think it over, this is a way of saying they don't want it. Most sales take place after five or six calls. It is a common error to think that you only need to call once. An objection to price generally means that you haven't convinced the person that you're the right person to buy from. Find out why.

Never mention price until the customer asks. When the price does come up, concentrate on linking it with value and benefits. Other ways of doing it are to compare the price to something else (to show what good value your product is) or to break the price down over a length of time (allowing the customer to pay in instalments).

■ **Closing the sale**
There are different ways of closing a sale:

- The direct close – ask for the order outright.

- The indirect close – 'You've got a lot to carry. I'm delivering in your area next week. Which day suits you best?' or 'Will this be cash or credit?'

- Summarize your presentation, concentrating on the benefits and ranking them in order.

- Summarize your presentation, listing the advantages and disadvantages. Then deal with the disadvantages.

- The alternative close – 'Which would you like, the red or the blue pair?'

- Let them take the product home to try it. (Make sure you have their address!)

- Tell them about another satisfied customer they can identify with.

- Start filling out the order form.

- 'You've made the right decision – would you like to sign here?'

- 'This is a special offer, not to be repeated.'

- 'Why aren't you placing the business with me?' (Then,

when you have found out the real reasons, go back and say 'If I dealt with that objection by doing . . . would you then buy from me?')

Planning your sales

You must set goals and know exactly how much you intend to earn. Money will only come from consistent hard work, and to be successful in selling you will need to be able to set yourself realistic and challenging goals. It is a good idea to link these to other goals, like paying the family mortgage and going on holiday! This means giving yourself annual income goals.

Define these goals in terms of the activities you must carry out in order to achieve them. Work out the sales volume needed to reach your required annual income, and then the monthly income and sales goals, weekly income and sales goals, daily income and sales goals, and the number of calls you need to make each day in order to achieve your goals.

Meeting these goals will require a great deal of determination, motivation and persistence. These are attributes that successful salespeople cannot do without.

You'll need to plan your sales very carefully. Set aside a certain number of hours or days for selling each week. Do this regularly and don't get yourself into the position of only having one customer.

Remember that you'll have to go back, on average, five or six times to make a sale. Some decisions take even longer to make. Be patient, don't panic and keep going.

EXAMPLE
Let's look at this example where the number of visits the salesperson has time to make is allocated to the customers in order of their importance to the business.

```
Days in the year     :    365
(less production)    :     75
(less weekends)     :    104
(less holidays)      :     15
(less sickness)      :      5
(less training)      :     10
(less conference)    :      5
(less meetings)      :     11
Total days          :    225
```

This leaves 140 days for selling (365 − 225 days).

Let's say you can do four visits in a day.

Now work out how many visits you can do in a year:
140 days × 4 visits = 560 visits a year.

Then work out who your customers will be and how much you
think you can sell each group:

Group	No. of Customers	No. of Sales	Income in £
A	10	10 000	100 000
B	100	1000	100 000
C	200	500	100 000
	310	11 500	300 000

Now decide how many times you need to visit each customer to
bring in the amount of money you want:

Group A: 12 visits a year
Group B: 3 visits a year
Group C: 1 visit a year

Then work out your total number of visits for the year:

Group A: 12 visits × 10 customers   = 120
Group B: 2 visits × 100 customers   = 200
Group C: 1 visit × 200 customers   = 200
                                       520

This figure gives you some flexibility, allowing for an extra 40 visits if necessary.

Find out where your customers are situated and plan your rota. Work out how much it will cost, taking into account all the overhead costs: petrol, fares, brochures, other sales aids, telephone, stamps, etc. Decide whether you can afford to carry out your plans, and change them if you have to. If you need help selling, consider using an agent or distributor. Contact the British Agents Register Ltd (see Useful addresses).

Selling through middlemen

If you want to sell through middlemen, you'll need to think about a number of factors:

- Coverage
  You will have to decide which types of shops would be best to sell in, how many you need, and where they will be located.

- Control
  You will need to ensure that you can cope with the extra administration, the extra production, delivery times, storage for raw materials and finished goods, and insurance requirements.

- Costs
  You will need to be able to afford the initial and continual cost; and you will need to make sure that your goods sell at the higher price necessary to allow for the middleman's mark-up, special trade discounts, display material, in-store and consumer promotions, haulage and packaging.

- Packaging
  You may need special packaging. This will need to be light, easy to handle and stack, and strong enough to protect the goods.

- Customer service
  You will have to work out a system to handle complaints, wrong invoices, short delivery, out-of-date goods, broken goods, and so on.

- Training
  It is unlikely that sales staff will sell your product to their customers unless you encourage them to do so. They may need training on how to sell your goods. And they will need to be encouraged and even rewarded as well.

- Display
  You will need to think about how you can get middlemen to display, price and promote your goods according to your requirements. You may have to get extra staff to help them arrange the goods.

- Stock control
  Think about the number of weeks' stock they should carry. How will they reorder and how often?

- Getting paid
  You will need to be able to chase up unpaid invoices and ensure you're paid on time. Have you thought about how long they will take to pay?

- Promotional material
  If middlemen produce a catalogue or price lists, how long are you expected to supply at the same price? Once you get your goods into the shops, you will need to encourage customers to go in and ask for them. Middlemen will not want shelves full of unsold goods; you'll need to convince them that your promotional methods will help them to sell your product.

12 Controlling your business

When you start your business you'll find that there won't be enough hours in the day to do everything. Most of your time will be spent getting business in and fulfilling orders. There will be precious little time left to sit down and think about what is actually happening. Life will appear as an endless stream of activities, and constant pressure will remove your ability to take a long term view of the business as a whole.

Common mistakes are:

- Neglecting to make sure that you have enough stock.
- Getting too much new work and not finishing off existing work so that you get a reputation for being unreliable.
- Not visiting new customers and quoting for new work.
- Delegating responsibility and neglecting to make sure that the work is being done properly.
- Not being able to produce enough.
- Not reaching the best standards.
- Charging too much or too little for your time.
- Forgetting to record orders and to send out invoices and statements.

- Not getting paid for all the work you have carried out.

- Not charging the optimum price.

- Paying more for materials and services than you need to.

- Not checking up on people before you give them any credit and also getting ripped off by unscrupulous people because you don't have enough time to reflect on what you're doing and what they might be getting up to. You will be surprised at the amount of paper work that is necessary to keep control of your business!

Identifying the key factors in controlling your business

When you start your own business you'll probably be so busy selling or working with other people during the day that most of your office work will have to be done over the weekends or at night.

As soon as possible you should sit down and think what the key issues will be in terms of controlling your business. Depending on your business, they could include achieving your required selling price, making full use of the hours you work, controlling the cost of stock, maintaining standards of quality, knowing how much to spend on advertising in order to keep the flow of work coming in, making sure you achieve the right profit margin, and so on. You may need to take advice from your accountant or Enterprise Agency.

Putting systems in place to control your business

Once you have decided what your key issues are, you will then have to work out a system of recording what is happening so that you can analyse the overall results at the end of the day, week or month. Try to make your systems easy to use, and get into the habit of using them from day one.

■ Office administration systems

Petty cash

Get some money from the bank and a petty cash voucher book and put this in a cash box. Every time you need some money for a small item that needs to be paid for in cash, fill in a voucher. When you have made your purchase, make sure you put the receipt back in the box with the voucher.

Telephone

Make sure your telephone is always manned during office hours and that you give the business name when you answer it. If you can't have someone there to answer the phone get an ansafone or a telephone answering service (be careful with these because once their number is on your business notepaper it will be difficult to change). You must also make sure that phone messages are taken properly. Get a proper pad that is always kept by the phone. Don't use scruffy bits of paper because they'll get lost. Think about your telephone manner. It is one of your most effective selling tools.

The telephone can also be used very successfully to remind your customers of any money they may owe you. If you're using it for debt collecting, just remember that it never pays to get angry with people. They could well react by making it even more difficult for you to get paid. Be polite but firm.

■ Recording orders

When you get an order from a customer, record it in a book straight away. Your record should include:

- Order number
- Date of order
- Name of customer, phone number and delivery address
- Description of goods
- Quantity ordered
- Value of order
- Delivery date

You will then be able to see how many orders you still have to do, which orders have been done, and how much these outstanding orders are worth.

There are other reasons for keeping accurate records of orders placed; in particular, to ensure that you eventually get paid. It may come as a shock when you first meet someone who is quite willing to accept your work and not pay you for it. If you haven't thought about this before, consider all the ways people can cheat on you before you part with your goods or services. Possible excuses include: never received the goods; never received the invoice; somebody else placed the order over the phone and they have left; never placed the order; the person who placed the order didn't have the authority; and so on.

For this reason, you need a system that proves the person sent the order (get a written order with an order number) and a method of delivery that makes it difficult to prove they did not receive the goods, so that you are able to claim nondelivery from the Post Office. Even better, get the money before you send the goods off. If they won't send the money in advance, don't send the goods. At least you won't be losing your money.

■ **Filling in job cards**
For some businesses a job card for each customer will help you check how many hours are being worked. You should record the following information:

- Job number
- Name of person carrying out the work
- Name of customer, address and phone number
- Customer's instructions
- Order date
- Completion date
- Work carried out
- Number of hours worked

- Price charged

- Volume and cost of materials used

- Any other information about the customer you think
  will be useful to you in the future

At the end of the week, month, or year, you could sit down and analyse the information you've recorded on the card. You would then be able to compare the different jobs completed and see who your best customers were (in terms of volume of work and price) and which months were the best months for your business.

A simple analysis form would summarize the information for each customer under the headings: date; job number; number of hours; price charged. If the invoice is over £100, the total (less VAT) and the VAT charged should also be shown.

Your job cards would also tell you how much time each person in the business was taking to carry out the work, how much money they were earning, and the volume and cost of the materials they were using. You could then use this information to see whether you were meeting your targets and also to review your business in other ways, asking questions such as: Are there any complaints? Could we do things more efficiently? Are our prices right? And so on.

■ **Keeping accounts**

Invoices
As soon as you have finished an order you must prepare and send out your invoice immediately. (You may have to enclose it with the goods or send it separately, according to the customer's requirements.) Think about the information you need to put on the invoice:

- Names of the owner/s, business address in Great
  Britain, and VAT number if VAT registered

- Name and address of customer

- Date and invoice number

- Description of goods ordered, quantity, value and order number
- Any extra charges for postage and/or delivery
- VAT if your business is VAT registered and the goods are standard rated
- Payment terms

ABC PRODUCTS

INVOICE

No MT 2746-2

26 Western Avenue
Kelminglon, West Bromley B44 27S
Tel 0477 221 677
Fax 0477 221 676

Firmin Industrial Services
Central Trading Estate
27 Bath Way
Bristol BS8 7DF

YOUR REF	QTY	DESCRIPTION OF GOODS	UNIT PRICE	DELIVERY	£
B2870	3	Amos Conditioners	£8.50	£3.00	£28.50
				TOTAL	28.50
				VAT AT 17.5%	4.98
				INVOICE TOTAL	33.48
TERMS 30 days					

Remember, the faster you send out your invoices the faster you will be paid. If possible, always ask for cash or a cheque (with cheque card number). If you can't get the money immediately, make sure you send your invoice to the person who initially placed the order. It is important to form a contact within the company. In companies with a large accounts department you should try to get the name of someone in the department so that they get to know you and take responsibility for ensuring that you get paid. Some people will find any excuse not to pay, or to delay paying so make sure there are no mistakes on your invoice and that it is reasonably close to your original estimate or matches the price quoted.

Keep all your invoices even before you start trading and remember to separate your paid invoices from your unpaid invoices.

Sales journal
When you send out your invoice you will need to record the customer's name, the amount you have invoiced for, the invoice number, the date of the invoice, and the date you actually get your money. If your bill is made up of parts and labour, you should record how the bill is split between them.

By recording this information in your sales journal, you can keep track of how quickly your invoices are being paid, and how long individual customers tend to take.

Customer account journal
If you have quite a few customers you may find it useful to have a special book in which you list them alphabetically, together with details of how much they owe you and when payment is due.

Statements
At the end of each month you should check the sales journal or customer account journal to see which invoices are still unpaid. You must then send a statement to each customer, listing all the invoices (by number and date) and the amounts that are still outstanding.

■ **Recording purchasing**
In most businesses a lot of money is tied up in stock – in other

words this money can't be used as cash until the stock has been sold and paid for. Examples could be materials that still need to be processed and finished products that need to be sold. The cost of keeping stock includes the purchase price, the interest on the money used to buy it, and the cost of warehousing or storage.

The longer you store stock, the greater the danger that it will deteriorate or get too old to use. Only purchase what you really need for confirmed orders or work in hand; it's too risky to carry stock on the offchance that you may get a suitable order for which to use it. The more often stock turns over in a year, the less money you will need to finance that stock, and the less interest you will be paying.

Stock control can be quite difficult in a shop because customers may want to see a wide range of goods on display. It is a matter of striking a balance between having what they need, and not loading the shelves with goods that you can't resist buying.

Purchase order forms

When you order stock, always keep a written note of what you have ordered and the terms and conditions you have specified, including delivery date. When you're busy it's tempting to ask someone to send you something and then put the matter aside because you feel it has now been dealt with. However you will find that many people accept work and then fail to do it. You therefore need a way of cancelling the order because legally they have broken their side of the agreement.

They may claim that they have already sent the goods (yesterday or last week). In that case you must question them very closely as to when they sent the package, where they sent it from, whether it was first or second class, Datapost, etc.

Always keep a record of the following:

- Purchase invoice number
- Supplier
- Total bill
  (Made up of)

- Precise requirements (so you can check if the quality is not up to standard)
- Order date
- Delivery date
- Payment terms
- Receipts (invoices)

Every receipt in connection with your business must be kept and filed. The whole point of keeping receipts is to prove to the taxman that you have made those purchases. Get two folders and keep a folder for receipts paid by petty cash and another for those paid by cheque. Receipts that are too small to file can be stuck on a plain piece of A4 paper. File the receipts for cheques in order of the cheque number with the cheque number written in the corner of each receipt. Receipts for petty cash should be filed in date order and numbered.

Purchase journal

This is similar to the sales journal but in it you write down the name of each supplier, the price and the day when payment is due. You can also record what goods and services you have bought under different headings so that you can see what you have bought and when. This will give you a running check on your spending and an opportuniy to check on your stock turnover, especially if you need to reduce your stock investment.

Your purchase journal should record the following information:

- Purchase invoice number
- Supplier
- Invoice date
- Total bill
  (Made up of)
- Date when payment is due
- Date paid
- Cheque number

Cash book

If you record your initial bank balance (bearing in mind your direct debits, e.g. gas and electricity bills) in your cash book you should be able to work out, from the information in the purchase and sales book, how much your bank balance is at the end of each day, week or month.

Your cash book will show two sets of information – money received and money paid out:

Money received
- Date money is received
- Sales invoice number
- Description of goods
- Receipt (cash in)
- Cash balance (bank only)

Money paid out
- Date money is paid
- Purchase invoice number
- Description of goods
- Cheque number
- Payment (cash out)
- Cash balance (bank only)

■ Producing accounts

You should be able to produce your monthly, quarterly and annual accounts from the information you have kept in your record books. You can then compare your projected income and expenditure with your actual accounts and see how successful you have been in achieving your objectives. Good accounts call for discipline and regular attention and there is no substitute for a sound financial system if you want to know exactly how the business is performing from one period to the next. It is a good idea to go on a basic book-keeping course. Alternatively, there are ready-made book-keeping packages that you can purchase from any shop selling office supplies.

■ **Getting paid**

When you do business with other companies you probably won't get paid immediately. Before giving credit you should always take some basic precautions: check your customer's legal identity and background; and establish a proper trading relationship.

Checking your customer's legal identity

As we have seen, there are three types of trading identity: sole traders, partnerships and limited companies. You may also find yourself doing business with other types of organizations, such as public limited companies (PLCS), local authorities, government agencies or voluntary unincorporated associations. Try to find out how these organizations deal with payments before doing any work for them. If you are at all unsure about their ability to pay you now, or in the future, ask them to provide the names and addresses of trade references, i.e. other firms who have done business with them. Follow up these references.

Dealing with sole traders

Sole traders are personally liable for the debts of their business. This means that, should their business fail their assets will be sold to pay the debts. If they lose all their money and have no assets you won't get paid. If you're at all unsure about a sole trader's ability to pay you now, or in the future, ask them to provide guarantors (individuals who know them and are prepared to pay the debt if necessary) or trade references from other organizations they have done business with.

Dealing with partnerships

The members of a partnership are jointly and severally liable for the debts of the partnership. They are in the same position as a sole trader, except that you can bring an action against any or all of the partners. Check their assets and ask them to provide guarantors. If something does go wrong and they don't pay, you could enforce a judgement against the partner who has the most assets.

Dealing with limited companies
Limited companies are separate legal entities. Although a company director must not allow a company to trade while it is insolvent, it is quite rare for a director to be forced to pay the debts incurred by the company.

Checking your customer's background
All limited companies have to give information about themselves to the Registrar of Companies at Companies House (see Useful addresses). Be careful, as this information (especially the accounts) is not always up to date. However it will have everything you need to know about the shareholders, directors, secretary, constitution, capital structure and registered office, the audited accounts, auditors' reports, directors' reports, mortgages and information about associated companies. You can either obtain this information yourself or ask a company registration agent to do it for you (see Useful addresses).

Things to look out for:

- Check whether the sole trader, any partner or those in charge of running the company are bankrupt. Although people who have been declared bankrupt cannot be directors of companies they may still be involved with their management. You can check the register of bankrupt persons kept by the Land Charges Department in Plymouth (see Useful addresses).

- Check whether any charges have been placed on the owner's property, such as a second mortgage.

- Check the Register of County Court Judgements to see whether any judgements have been recorded against them (see Useful addresses).

- Visit their premises and see what sort of place it is. Is it a genuine address or merely a front?

Credit reference agencies
Credit reference agencies can make other checks to find out whether people are likely to default on their debts. Find a local

agency (see Useful addresses), as they will have information on
bankruptcies, County Court Judgements, other searches and
details of other defaults. They would also be able to get you trade
references and tell you what information you would need to get
from Companies House, and advice on how to enforce judgement
debts.

Establishing a proper trading relationship
You can establish a proper trading relationship with your
customers by drawing up a contract (see Chapter 5). Using correct
and effective procedures is vital from the start.

Many small businesses don't have a great number of clients.
Business relationships must therefore be treasured and looked
after. This means that if you offend a client by handling your
requests for payment badly or – even worse – a customer absconds
without paying, the damage to your business can be quite
catastrophic.

If you're sending goods by post it is preferable to ask for payment
before you send them. If you're providing a service try and get
some or all of the money before you carry out the job. You ought
at least to obtain an advance to pay for materials for the job. Try
not to buy materials for customers on your account. Asking for
money before you deliver the goods may sound difficult, but it is
far better to lose an order than to waste time performing the
service or making the goods and then not get paid for it. You can
also consider asking for payment in instalments.

Monitor your transactions all the time. For example, photocopying
the cheques may make you realize that a customer is changing
bankers very frequently (which could be a sign of financial
problems). Work out a system that proves a customer sent an
order (get a written order with an order number). And use a
method of delivery where it is difficult for customers to prove that
they never received the goods. In genuine cases of loss, this will
enable you to claim non-delivery from the Post Office.

■ **How to make a customer pay**
Your terms of trading and your invoice will have stated when you

expect to be paid (30 days is the most common period). Make sure that you send out statements as soon as payment is due. If this doesn't work, phone the customer to remind them. (If you wish, you can call beforehand to tell them that you're about to send your bill.) When you ask for money, never suggest that you think there may be a problem. You have to motivate your customers and encourage them to pay. This means that you must be charming and not be tempted to threaten them because a negative attitude will make the situation even more tense. Even if you know they are outright scoundrels, never let your opinion show.

Before you phone, make sure that you have all the records in front of you so that you're prepared for any disagreements. Write down everything they say and keep a note of the date of each conversation. In this way you can build up a portfolio of evidence which you can use in court if necessary. Give them a date that you expect to be paid by, and if the payment doesn't arrive, telephone them again and again. Keep telephoning and keep being pleasant.

If this doesn't work, write a letter stating that you will institute County Court proceedings if payment is not received by another deadline. Ask your local County Court for their literature on how to use the small claims procedure. But do not make threats unless you really mean to carry them out and always seek legal advice before starting an action. Your Enterprise Agency should be able to recommend a good solicitor. This is when legal expenses insurance cover becomes very cost-effective. You could also use a debt-collecting service.

Quality

You may need to demonstrate to your customers that you are committed to quality. BS5750 is the UK National Standard Quality System; it is the same as the International Standard ISO 9000. Having a BS5750 Certification Mark and being included in the Quality Register of the Department of Trade and Industry should improve your marketing opportunities. Take advice about this from your Enterprise Agency.

13 Managing yourself

Changing your role from an employed person to that of a self-employed person is perhaps one of the most difficult and challenging tasks you'll have to face in your journey towards creating your own successful business. People who have worked for years in the same company sometimes develop what is called an 'employee mentality', this is also spoken of as carrying out a 'mindless activity', one in which the person is not having to think and feel about the meaning of the relationship between themselves and their work.

Each person entering self-employment brings their own past experiences and their own fantasies about what this new life will involve. Work helps us to define our identity in relation to the outside world. The type of work we do gives other people an idea of who we are. When we first meet someone, along with the question, 'What is your name?' goes the question, 'What do you do?'

Changing your work role involves changing not only your own perception of yourself but also the way you are perceived by other people in that your sociological role has changed from an employed person to a self-employed person. Becoming a self-employed person (rather than an employee) inevitably changes what people expect from you (both overtly and covertly) and may isolate you at first from friends, family and former colleagues.

Self-employment also involves a change in your psychological role, enabling you to see yourself as an independent person with your own power and authority. Your success will very much depend on how you manage yourself in your new role: how other people view you; how you view yourself; and how much you can extend yourself.

Working in the over-protected and stultifying environment of a large company for too long can sometimes destroy initiative and independence. Fortunately, this problem is well recognized and if you find yourself being made redundant after working for many years in such a job, there are plenty of training courses and support groups around to help you to rediscover your sense of power, initiative, drive and authority. Ask your local Training Enterprise Council (TEC) or Enterprise Agency. Being your own boss will also give you the opportunity to structure your own environment and create meaning for yourself.

Develop your role

It is important to think about the reasons why you want to become self-employed and to reflect seriously on whether you have the imagination and the ability to create a self-employed role for yourself and the scale on which you want to create it. Think about your feelings. For example, with some people the mere thought of calling themselves, 'Managing Director', is enough to make them quiver! Try saying 'I am the Managing Director' or 'I am the Chairman'. How does it make you feel?

The word 'role', in this sense, implies something that you're going to create or discover within yourself; something that is part of you and yet separate from you. In order to get to grips with any difficulties you may have in carrying out this role, you need to develop a sense of objectivity about it.

It is rather like taking on the role of parenting: you can look at the job you're doing and say, 'As a parent I need to be more understanding with my children.' Looking at your self-employed role in this way will allow you to be more objective about what you're doing, so that the stresses and strains don't impact on to you personally and you're able to analyse and criticize your actions in order to become more effective. Think about the feelings and thoughts that will go through your mind when you play your role, and any anxieties or defences you may be building up which will prevent you from doing your work properly. Anxieties which also come from carrying out the work itself which in some cases can be quite unpleasant.

Part of the pleasure and part of the difficulty lies in the fact that your business is a unique expression of you. You are the business; and as people tend to create their environments, including their business organizations, as mirror images of themselves, it is often extremely difficult to take an objective position and ensure that your business reflects what your customers need, rather than your own self-image. It very frequently does not say what you think it is saying!

EXAMPLE
Michael decided he would start his own business after a few lean and very painful years. He had been made redundant a couple of times and was finding it difficult to get another job. As a last resort, he had some business cards printed and booked himself in for a class on promotion. His business card was printed on cheap paper, his name was in minute print and he had left out his professional qualifications; no one even knew what he did. After some time it was possible to bring up the subject of his low self-image. He was asked to think about what his business card was telling people. As soon as he started to reflect on it, he realized that he hadn't created a role. Instead, he had developed a business image that told everyone how awful he felt about himself and his life. Fortunately, he went on to create something more positive that was related to the market and the role his customers' wanted him to play in order for their needs to be satisfied.

■ The golden rules of self-employment

■ **Adapt to the market**
In creating your role you must always take the market into consideration. This will determine what other people expect from

you. You have to look at your role within the context in which you'll be working. It is all too easy to do what you want to do, or what you think the market needs, without ever checking to see whether you're right.

When you create meaning for yourself every act of creation will involve you in your own internal world. At first you'll create images and ideas that will make you feel great, but the next minute you'll plunge to the depths of despair when you realize they won't work in the market. As time passes you'll slowly be able to take your ideas out of your head and mould them into an external reality, rather like making a piece of sculpture. All the time you'll need to keep careful control of the interplay between your internal world of fantasy and the external world of facts. Nothing ever exists in a vacuum and you need to position yourself, your business and your product/service in relation to what is already in the market.

EXAMPLE
Joe had a good idea for a burglar alarm system; the market was growing and he saw no reason why he shouldn't take a share of it. He thought he had a brilliant name for his company and, without registering it, or even checking to see whether anybody else was using it (even when he was instructed to), he spent several thousand pounds on sales material. A few months later he was at an exhibition and two aisles away was a company with exactly the same name. Well, one of them had to destroy their literature and change their name. As the other company had protected their name, poor Joe, with his limited capital, was the one. He almost went out of business.

■ **Create objectives**
If you have clear personal objectives and a realistic sense of your strengths and weaknesses, this should help you formulate your tasks and decide on what you can and cannot do. The ability to distinguish between fantasy and reality must be constantly maintained and developed as you adapt to changing conditions.

Creating objectives is rather like throwing a ball across a field – unless you throw the ball you won't know how far to run. Unless you know what you want to achieve you won't know how big or small your business should be, or even how hard you should work. This will also help you decide on your legal form – sole trader, partner, limited company or cooperative – and whether you want to employ people or work with them on a temporary or associate basis. It will also have some influence on the type of markets and money you go for, and the way you develop your promotional programme.

■ **Know what you want**
It is very important to have a clear idea of what you want out of your venture. If some of the things you want are unexpressed, you may find these unconscious drives determining how you spend your money.

EXAMPLE
Jane cared a great deal about status. She came from a family where money had been short and she needed to feel that she was an important person. Setting herself up as the director of a limited company made her feel important even though it was not strictly necessary in view of the size of her turnover, the element of risk, the money she needed to raise, or the context in which she worked. She bought an expensive car, had a telephone answering service, employed an expensive accountant and solicitor, bought a computer and paid a secretary. Needless to say, her search for status, and an impressionable and over-generous bank manager, got her into enormous debt.

■ **Have the right attitude**
Overwhelming optimism tempered with commonsense (or, rather, uncommon sense) is the best attitude for the self-employed person. There are no get-rich-quick schemes that really work and if you have a childlike belief in other people and are easily strung along, self-employment is not an option for you – until you become more realistic. The university of life can do it for you, but at great financial and emotional cost. Read the real-life examples below. Do they ring a bell?

The utopia syndrome
The joy of being your own boss can make you think you have found total fulfilment. The may lead you into setting unattainable utopian goals, such as constant happiness and success. This is dangerous . . .

Everything you dream up must have its potential assessed. You may have luck on your side, but there again, you may not. In the beginning, self-employed people consistently overestimate their sales and place too much trust in other people.

EXAMPLE
Jack was always chasing the next rainbow. He never wanted to investigate or be realistic about the various business propositions that were offered to him by so-called 'friends'. His attitude was that they were jolly nice fellows to include him. It was only when one of them went to jail for fraud that the penny finally dropped. Jack suffered a partial collapse, lost all ambition and faith in himself, and drifted from job to job getting nowhere.

You should never allow yourself to think that all your problems will be over once you reach your goal. The only happy-ever-after endings are in fairy tales. Change always involves discomfort, disappointment and difficulty and your journey into self-employment will be no different from any other process of transition.

The procrastination syndrome
Robert Louis Stevenson said, 'It is better to journey hopefully than to arrive.' But some people never actually go forward to do anything. Instead they go on endlessly researching or fiddling around with their ideas. Research is important but don't use it as an excuse for not taking the plunge and actually starting up in business.

EXAMPLE
Jennifer lived in a fairly affluent town where a large number of residents had travelled abroad and acquired a taste for fine chocolate. She decided to set up a business making chocolates and

went on a course to find out more about self-employment. She finished the course and everyone thought she was well on her way. However almost eight months later she went on another course. When asked why she was there, she said that it was such a complicated subject she was still deciding on the flavours, the packaging, the numbers to be packed into each box and so on.

■ Don't only do what you enjoy

You may experience a tendency only to do the things you enjoy.

EXAMPLE

Peter liked writing computer programs and found selling very difficult; he was shy and unassuming and disliked approaching people uninvited. Instead of facing his difficulties and getting some training, he kept putting it off. As a result he didn't make enough calls and was slowly going out of business (although he had a large stock of computer programs). It wasn't until he found someone to make the initial business appointments for him that he realized that he could sell. All he needed was someone to help him over the first hurdle.

■ Don't let failure get you down

If you are going to work on your own, you must be able to cope with failure. See it as a chance to learn from your mistakes and make sure you get the right help and advice next time round. Many people start and fail and then try again. The skills they have acquired the first time round stand them in good stead. They gradually go through the hard school for entrepreneurs and learn by their mistakes. Once you get the hang of it, there should be no stopping you.

Some words of warning

- You must learn how to check people out and not necessarily trust them.

- You may lose money if you do not succeed.

- You have to learn how to walk away from failure and very often debt.

- You may have to learn how to use other people's money and not your own to finance your ideas.

- You may find it difficult to raise the money and be driven into borrowing money from the wrong people.

- You may have to work long hours and have little free time. Some self-employed people enjoy this but rest is important and driving yourself to complete exhaustion will destroy you and ultimately your business.

- You may have no regular income to begin with.

- You must be prepared to learn something about everything.

- You must be willing to do certain things you dislike.

- You will have to learn to balance effort with income and not waste time on unimportant, unprofitable tasks.

■ Other areas you must pay attention to

■ **Reactions from your family**
Your family will also have to live with your new role and they may not be quite as excited about it as you are.

EXAMPLE
Bill was an experienced trainer. He decided when he took early retirement that he would join a consortium of loosely associated trainers and work freelance. However his wife couldn't bear the uncertainty of his irregular timetable. Consequently the marriage became extremely stressed and he finally gave up and took a job at a local college with regular working hours.

This sort of reaction may well appear irrational, but your change in status will also affect your partner's feelings about who they are and where they stand in the world. Their expectations of you may be largely unconscious, until they are faced with the 'new you'. Your partner and your family may well have to change their ideas about what Mum or Dad can do. It will be very difficult if your own family don't support your plans. But you can understand their concern if the money you need to print your brochure or purchase machinery can only be found by increasing the mortgage on the family home!

■ **Reactions from friends and former colleagues**
Human beings are social creatures; we live and work with groups of people. These groups give us a sense of identity and a feeling of security. By becoming self-employed, you become something different. And the only way most people are able to deal with difference is to denigrate it. Some people might start asking, 'Would no one else give him/her a job?' If they have this sort of attitude it is unlikely that you'll be able to make customers of them and it's best to put their opinions out of your mind.

You may find it helpful to join a business club (for social and business contacts) and be seen doing something for the community (you can make this part of your public relations plan). Donating money to charity, sponsoring an event, supporting the arts, chairing a committee or giving talks free of charge, are all ways of making a contribution. As a person with their own business, you can now play an active role in helping to create wealth.

On the other hand if you're dealing with people who have an 'employee mentality', they may think that self-employment just gives you an excuse to have an easier life. You may be viewed with envy and resentment. Envy is a fact of life and it is something to be aware of. So don't talk about your wonderful holidays in the Bahamas (when and if you get them!). It will only confirm their suspicions.

■ **Keeping a sense of perspective**
The increased responsibility of taking your own decisions can lead to a greater sense of anxiety. New situations may also reveal aspects of yourself that are less easy to deal with, such as fear, depression, greed, laziness, lack of motivation and irrational anger when other people don't play the game (like not paying your invoices). Some tasks will be unpleasant, such as getting rid of a business partner or asking for money. You may even find yourself crying and begging for money from customers and bank managers – it has been known to happen!

These stresses and strains can make it impossible to ask for help. They also make it difficult to analyse and evaluate results and look at yourself and your actions and achievements objectively and in the long term. It's easy to get paranoid and think that you can't check anything out because someone will copy you. It's even easier to get to the point where you don't want to analyse your sales receipts for fear of finding out that you have failed.

EXAMPLE
Brian went on a course on selling. He was an experienced salesperson in his fifties. When asked what was wrong he said the business was just not coming in, and he was sure there was something wrong with his sales techniques. He was asked for an analysis of his sales by customer and by area, and for a breakdown of his advertising to sales ratios over the past three years. Amazingly he had no analysed record of his sales, he had no idea of how many calls he had to make to get a sale, and he had no idea of who his most profitable customers were. All he knew was that his turnover was dropping! Are you surprised? Sadly, he was so defensive that even when he was asked to provide this information he resisted it. Fear can make people behave in self-destructive ways.

You have to learn how to play the business game, in the same way that a footballer must remember he is playing a game. If a footballer forgets the rules and begins to punch and kick he has lost his sense of reality. When this happens he has lost the game, and so it is in business. You must follow the rules and get to know about the established ways of running a business, they have been developed for very good reasons.

How do we know whether we are going to make mistakes like these? The answer is that we don't know until we actually start making them and then is the time to talk to as many knowledgeable, objective people as we can. Don't go and ask someone who will agree with everything you say. You need honest advice you can weigh up and decide to follow or ignore. Always seek out the best advice, although the final decision will be yours.

Plan and acquire the skills that will enable you to make the transition to self-employment relatively smoothly. Above all, be honest with yourself.

■ **Developing an organizational system**
Becoming a successful self-employed person means developing an organizational system. This will consist of:

- A marketing system to help you adapt to the environment and keep getting the work.
- A disciplined, quality-driven task system to keep producing the work.
- An accurate financial system to keep track of costs and profitability.

In order to keep these sub-systems working well you need a constant flow of work coming in and going out, and the flow going out should help more work to come in. Most customers, if they have a bad experience, will not come back. And what is more, they will never tell you about it; they will just tell other people. You have to find out why they were dissatisfied because it costs a lot more to get a new customer than it takes to keep an existing customer. Continue your market research all the time.

■ **Extending your role**
Once you start your business you'll have to perform a variety of roles and carry out a multitude of different tasks. These roles and tasks will require different skills and abilities, especially the ability to behave and think in a variety of different ways. For example, to take the role of a salesperson, you need to learn how to enact it and be confident in your ability to sell. You have to understand the culture and the context in which that role is carried out.

Try saying, 'I am a salesperson', or 'I can write letters, copy, news releases', or 'I am a book-keeper', or 'I can speak in public'. Watch your feelings and what comes into your mind when you make such statements. Then work on anything that will prevent you from carrying out that role effectively, such as lack of the appropriate skills, lack of confidence, anxieties, lack of knowledge and so on.

Performing a selling role requires different tasks and behavioural skills from those required by your book-keeping role. All these different roles need to be broken down into a time framework and only performed when your mind is wholly on them. Don't try and shift tasks and roles all the time. Separate them and make sure you don't get confused. Don't try and sell and do your book-keeping at the same time; both tasks require you to concentrate and think about yourself in different ways. Structure your day around your roles and allocate specific periods of time for each one. Time management is very important for self-employed people. You may find it helpful to go on a course and your Enterprise Agency should have information on these or you can get various books on this subject.

It will take time to understand the tasks and roles you need to develop in order to achieve your objectives. Don't expect to be able to achieve complete stability from day one. It has been said that starting your own business is like asking someone who knows nothing about music to write a concerto. It takes a mature person to create and maintain a self-motivating, reflective position in which they can conduct the cacophony of sounds and confusing impulses coming from within themselves. However, it can be very exciting!

If you find that you're unable to carry out all these different roles and tasks yourself you'll still have to ensure that they are carried out. You could go on self-development courses or you could use outside help or work with someone whose skills complement your own. You could also employ someone to carry out the work for you. Do remember that you can't do everything yourself and it is often well worth spending the money to pay a professional to carry out some aspects of the work for you. You can also form a relationship with a process consultant or a management consultant. This will help you with your decision-making and will give you a form of supervision at the same time.

■ **Adjusting to self-employment**
Think about the aspects of organizational life that you may feel you'll miss: regular pay, fixed hours with weekends or other time to yourself, holiday and sick pay, security, pension, possible bonuses and profit-sharing schemes, support from colleagues, supervision and so on. Some of these are essential, like sick pay, a

pension and insurance. These you must now purchase for yourself. Others may not appear to be essential at first. For example, social life and support from colleagues may not seem that important, but once you have experienced days on end working by yourself you may find it useful to replace this network in some other way.

Shared decision-making, the setting of objectives, supervision and the structuring of time are other important elements which you'll now have to manage on your own.

On the whole, working within an organization allows for the sharing and specialisation of roles and tasks. Working with other people allows you (on the whole) to do what you like doing and are good at. It protects you from the real world and enables you to create a world for yourself that is often unrelated to the conditions of the market and the harsh realities of life. Self-employment does not give you this protection. You must at all times keep your entire organizational system in mind, not only the part you happen to like doing! This means holding all the sub-systems in your mind.

Organizations also provide people with a framework within which they can allocate blame. If something goes wrong you can say it was another person's fault or another department's responsibility. You can walk away from it all when you go home and leave all your bad feelings at work. Many self-employed people, however, work by themselves at home and find it difficult to 'switch off'. It is important to create a strict boundary between your work role and your role as a family member.

■ Looking to the future

■ Expanding your business
Too much work and too little time to do it will result in lost sales opportunities, production problems, missed deliveries, quality control problems and cash flow difficulties. Your time will be devoted to controlling the business and you'll have less time available to anticipate problems and opportunities. You may then need to grow. This will mean having to employ people, get larger premises, buy more plant, create an organizational structure with proper job descriptions and raise more money.

In order to take your business into this stage of growth and maturity you will have to be prepared to eliminate virtually your own role within the sub-systems. This is difficult, as it takes enormous maturity to take on the problem of succession and face the loss of control involved. You will need to decide how big you want the company to grow, and you will have to consider all over again what you really want.

Instead of incorporating and performing a multitude of roles and tasks, you will now have to disengage from a number of them in order to allow an organizational structure to emerge, with other people performing the tasks you previously carried out.

Many of the feelings that drove you into self-employment, such as the sense of powerlessness and lack of control that you had in employment or unemployment, will begin to raise their nasty heads again. By then your business will have become a statement of success. This will have an emotional significance for you that other people will find hard to understand. Your business will have become a reality that you personally have created and one that you'll expect other people to cherish in the same way as you. Sadly, others will never have the same sense of excitement about your achievements as you will. An employee's relationship with somebody else's organization is never the same as it is with his own. You'll then have to face the realities of organizational life all over again and learn how to manage yourself in a different role, because by then you will be managing people.

A desire to keep control can lead a lot of entrepreneurs into running their businesses in a very autocratic way. Rather like a spider in the middle of a web they occupy a central place within the organization, from which all commands are issued. There is very little delegation or planning. Roles and tasks are eroded from the centre and people who come into the organization will probably be yes-men and anyone who challenges the authority of the entrepreneur may not be allowed to stay on. The culture is highly political.

Behaviour like this will seriously threaten the future of the business. The entrepreneur will need to stabilize the situation by developing a proper organizational structure and decision-making process so that the business is properly equipped to deal with the external world and determine its priorities. Finance will need to be arranged to help the business grow, and manpower recruited and trained so that the business continues to market a quality product or service. If this is impossible, it may be better, rather than destroying the business, to sell it or let someone else run it and start something new.

Growth needs to be planned for, and you may want to look at different types of financing such as bringing in shareholders. Business plans need to be written and the product or service portfolio will need to be evaluated so that markets can be properly exploited or expanded. You may want to think about diversification or acquisition. Personnel policies need to be implemented and employees will need to be rewarded and motivated. All this will involve you in a host of different activities, none of which you probably thought you would ever take on!

■ **When things go wrong. . .**
Things are bound to go wrong at some stage or another and it would be unrealistic to think that they won't. All you can do is think about your objectives and try to plan ahead. Make sure that you give yourself enough time to think things through properly. If you have a hunch, it may be a good one or it may be a bad one. Try and tolerate the frustration of not doing anything about it until you can think more objectively. Do nothing in haste and always sleep on it before making a decision.

When things go wrong, start by defining the problem correctly. Do not deny that a problem exists or convince yourself that it will go away if you ignore it. Don't over-simplify it either, because by doing so you may ignore its complexity, come to the wrong conclusion and apply the wrong solution. (There is the old story of the drunk who has lost his keys and is found looking for them under a lamp-post. When asked why he is looking for them there, he replies, 'Because that is where the light is best.')

Try not to put your head in the sand and think that if you don't look up all your problems will go away. Don't develop tunnel vision. Try to look around you, rather than straight ahead. Be truthful and objective about yourself and what you and your business are achieving. If you feel in your bones that something is going wrong, don't deny your instincts and observations, however unwelcome they may be. Put them in front of someone else and discuss them. Try to work out whether they are unrealistic anxieties or a reality you must deal with. If necessary, pay a professional, such as your accountant, management consultant or process consultant, to help you do this.

■ **Try, try, try again**
If you don't succeed the first time try again. You will have learnt a few lessons by now, and failure is as much part of business as success. Even large successful businesses make mistakes; the only difference between them and you is that they can probably afford to make them. Starting a business is fairly easy – staying in business is more difficult. Success is a chancy affair. I hope the information in this book will make your progress a little smoother. Good luck and enjoy yourself, at least some of the time!

Useful addresses

Advertising Association (Aslib)
(*The Marketing Pocket Book 1993* is available from NTC Publications)
Abford House, 15 Wilton Road, London, SW1V 1LT
Tel: 071 828 2771/4831 *Fax*: 071 931 0376

Association for Information Management
Information House, 20–40 Old Street, London, EC1V 9AP
Tel: 071 253 4488 *Fax*: 071 430 0514

Banking Information Service
10 Lonbard Street, London, EC3V 9AT
Tel: 071 626 8486/9386 *Fax*: 071 283 7037

British Agents Register
24 Mount Parade, Harrogate, North Yorkshire, HG1 1BP
Tel: 0423 560608/9 *Fax*: 0423 561204

British Franchise Association
Thames View, Newton Road, Henley-on-Thames, Oxfordshire,
RG9 1HG
Tel: 0491 578050 *Fax*: 0491 572517

British Insurance & Investment Brokers Association
14 Bevis Marks, London, EC3 7LH
Tel: 071 623 9043 for a list of local brokers *Fax*: 071 626 9676

British Library Science Reference and Information Service
25 Southampton Buildings, London, WC2A 1AW
Tel: 071 323 7485 *Fax*: 071 323 7482

Central Statistical Office
Government Buildings, Cardiff Road, Newport, Gwent, NP9 1XG
Tel: 0633 812973 *Fax*: 0633 812599

Chamber of Commerce
Look in the *Yellow Pages* for your local chamber

Companies House
Companies House, Crown Way, Maindy, Cardiff, CF4 3UZ
Tel: 0222 388588 *Fax*: 0222 380900

Company Registration Agents
Consult *Yellow Pages* for your nearest agent, or ask your solicitor or accountant for a recommendation

Company Searches
Consult *Yellow Pages* for your nearest Company Registration Agent

Construction Industry Training Board
Bircham Newton, King's Lynn, Norfolk, PE31 6RH
Tel: 0553 776677 *Fax*: 0553 692226

Co-Operatives
Phone ICOM 0532 461738 for information and details of your nearest agency dealing with co-operatives

County Courts
Look in *Yellow Pages* under Courts

Credit Reference Agencies
Look in *Yellow Pages* under Credit Reference Agencies

Credit Investigation Agencies
Look in *Yellow Pages* under Credit Investigation Services

Customs & Excise
Look in *Yellow Pages* for the nearest office

Data Protection Registrar
PO Box 66, Wilmslow, Cheshire, SK9 5AX
Tel: 0625 535777

Department of Employment
Look in the local telephone directory under Employment Service

Department of Social Security
Look in the local telephone directory under Social Security

Department of Trade and Industry
Ashdown House, Victoria Street, London, SW1
Tel: 071 215 5000 for general enquiries or look up your nearest office in the local telephone directory under DTI: Department of Trade and Industry

Debt-Collecting Agencies
Look in *Yellow Pages* under Debt Collectors

Direct Marketing Association (UK)
Haymarket House, 1 Oxendom Street, London, SW1Y 4EE
Tel: 071 321 2525 *Fax*: 071 321 0191

Enterprise Agency Trust (for Scotland)
Look in *Yellow Pages* for your nearest office

Environmental Health Office
Consult your local District Council

European Commission
Tel: 071 973 1992 *Fax*: 071 973 1900
Ask for Information Centre

Euromonitor Publications Ltd
87 Turnmill Street, London, EC1M 5QU
Tel: 071 251 8024 *Fax*: 071 608 3149

Export Credits Guarantee Department
50 Ludgate Hill, London EC4

HMSO Books
St Crispins, Duke Street, Norwich, NR3 1PD
Tel: 0603 62211

Industrial Training Boards
Check your local library for the relevant board

Inland Revenue
Look in the local telephone directory for your nearest office

Institute of Marketing
Moor Hall, Cookham, Bucks., SL6 9QH
Tel: 0628 524922 *Fax*: 0628 531382

Land Charges Department
Drake's Hill Court, Burrington Way, Plymouth, PL5 3LP
Tel: 0752 779831 *Fax*: 0752 766666

Law Society
Ipsley Court, Barrington Close, Redditch, Worcs., B98 0TD
Tel: 0527 517141
Ask for a list of local solicitors who participate in the Lawyers For
Enterprise Scheme

Local Council
Look them up in your local telephone directory

Local Investment Networking Co. (LINC)
4 Snow Hill, London, EC1A 2BS
Tel: 071 236 3000 *Fax*: 071 329 0226

NTC Publications
Farm Road, Henley-on-Thames, Oxfordshire, RG9 1EJ
Tel: 0491 574671 (written orders only accepted for *The Marketing Pocket Book*)

Offshore Petroleum Industry Training Organisation Ltd
Forties Road, Montrose, Angus, DD10 9ET
Tel: 0224 872058 *Fax*: 0224 249459

Register of County Court Judgements
Registry Trust Limited, 173–175 Cleveland Street, London, W1P 5PE
Tel: 071 380 0133 *Fax*: 071 388 0672

RTITB Services Ltd
Capitol House, Enterprise Way, Wembley, Middlesex, HA9 0NG
Tel: 081 902 8880 *Fax*: 081 903 4113

Trade Association Head Office
Check your local library for details of the relevant association

Training and Enterprise Council
Look in the local telephone directory

Venture Capital Report Ltd
Boston Road, Henley-on-Thames, Oxfordshire, RG9 1DY
Tel: 0491 579999